Report of the Expert Committee

Review of the Mental Health Act 1983

November 1999

CONTENTS

APPENDICES

Chair of Expert Committee

Genevra Richardson - Professor of Public Law, Queen Mary and Westfield College, University of London.

Membership of Expert Committee

Ros Alstead - Director of Nursing & Quality / Director of Operations, South Birmingham Mental Health NHS Trust

William Bingley - Chief Executive of Mental Health Act Commission

Anne Bird - Consultant Psychiatrist - Royal Free Hospital

Jenny Goodall - Head of Community Care, Royal Borough of Kensington & Chelsea

Rodney Lind QPM - Deputy Chief Constable - Wiltshire Constabulary
Represented by:

Detective Chief Inspector
Paul Howlett
Sergeant Robert Pack

Robert Mather - General Practitioner - North Oxford Medical Centre. Appointed Mental Health Act Commissioner 1997

Grainne McMorrow - Barrister, specialist in Mental Health Law. Mental Health and Legal Policy Consultant

David Ndegwa - Consultant Forensic Psychiatrist. Clinical Director in Forensic Psychiatry - South London & The Maudsley NHS Trust

Jill Peay - Senior Lecturer in Law – London School of Economics.
Barrister

Nigel Pleming QC   -   Barrister, practising in Public Law and special interest in Mental Health Law. Vice Chair of Mental Health Act Commission Jan 1995-Dec 1996

David Shiers   -   Carer - daughter with severe mental health problems. General Practitioner. Primary Care Lead for West Midlands Partnership in Mental Health

SUMMARY

1. This summary follows the structure of the Report. It aims to cover the principal issues raised. These will appear under the headings used in the Report for the ease of cross referencing.

INTRODUCTION

2. The Committee was commissioned to advise on how mental health legislation should be shaped to reflect contemporary patterns of care within a framework which balances the need to protect the rights of individual patients and the need to ensure public safety. The Committee has been primarily concerned with providing a framework for compulsion in respect of certain people with mental disorder and, within the time constraints imposed, it is satisfied that it has devised a structure capable of delivering modern mental health care in a way which is acceptable to those whose co-operation is crucial to the successful implementation of policy. However, the Committee is very aware of the complexity of the issues involved and urges government to engage in extensive further consultation.

GENERAL PRINCIPLES

3. The desire to promote the principle of non-discrimination on grounds of mental ill health has been fundamental to the Committee's approach, and this has led to an emphasis on patient autonomy. The Committee recommends the inclusion within new legislation of statements of principle which will set the tone of the new act and guide its interpretation. Principles to be expressed include informal care, the provision of the least restrictive alternative compatible with the delivery of safe and effective care, consensual care, reciprocity, respect for diversity and the recognition of the role of carers.

The Code of Practice

4. The Committee is keen to enhance the authority of the Code of Practice and makes recommendations as to how this might be achieved, including an express statutory presumption of compliance.

ENTITLEMENTS

5. The Committee is convinced that if society is to impose a duty to comply with care and treatment on some of those who suffer from mental disorder it must impose a parallel duty on health and social care authorities to provide an appropriate standard of care and treatment for those subject to compulsion. However, the Committee is concerned that this principle of

reciprocity should not result in diverting resources from informal care. The report therefore recommends measures to ensure that a balance is struck between the quality of care provided to informal and compelled patients.

Rights which Flow from Compulsion

6.   The Committee recommends a number of specific rights to be accorded to patients under compulsion. In addition to the right to receive the approved care and treatment and ongoing care for a determined period, these rights would include, at the earliest possible opportunity, the right to advocacy, the right to information about and assistance with drawing up an advance agreement and, for those detained in hospital, the right to safe containment consistent with respect for human dignity. With regard to the right to receive care and treatment including ongoing care after a period of compulsion, the Committee makes some specific recommendations and emphasises the need for a comprehensive review of charging policy.

Access to Services

7.   The Committee recommends the introduction of both a user's right to an assessment of mental health needs, and a carer's right to request such an assessment.

The Protection of Remaining Civil Liberties

8.   The Committee recommends measures designed to ensure that no further deprivation of liberty is imposed on the patient under compulsion save that which is expressly authorised by the legislation or is necessarily implied by the need to achieve safe containment.

THE SCOPE OF COMPULSION

9.   In seeking to define those people who should come within the scope of the compulsory framework the Committee adopts the following approach: a broad diagnostic criterion with some express exclusions, coupled to rigorous entry criteria, the strictness of which increases as the patient progresses from assessment to a compulsory order.

The Diagnostic Criterion

10.   The Committee favours retaining the term 'mental disorder' and including a broad definition within the act. Reference to specific definitional schemes should be made in the Code of Practice.

11. While the Committee recommends dropping the term 'psychopathic disorder' from any new act, it assumes personality disorders will be included within the broad definition of mental disorder and does not wish to see them expressly excluded.

12. In making recommendations concerning people with longterm incapacity the Committee faced considerable difficulties. The Committee does not consider that a mental health act is the appropriate framework for such people. There is an urgent need to provide a comprehensive statutory framework specifically designed for people with longterm incapacity, and the Committee urges the government to make the necessary provision. However, because the Committee considers there will be some people with learning disability who will require care and treatment under a mental health act, it does not recommend that learning disability be expressly excluded from the scope of the new mental health act.

THE STRUCTURE OF COMPULSORY POWERS

13. The Committee accepts that there will be a need for compulsory assessment powers when attempts to provide informal care and treatment have failed. Accordingly it recommends that authority to impose compulsory assessment lies, as at present, in the hands of three mental health professionals. For the time being it accepts that an ASW should continue to be the applicant, but it recommends that thought be given to extending the role to include other mental health professionals who are not psychiatrists.

14. The criteria for admission to assessment should reflect those required for the eventual imposition of a compulsory order and the application should be based on objective grounds. The order should last for a maximum of 7 days, during which time a series of assessments would have to be conducted. 'Formal' rather than 'compulsory' assessment would be available in the community. Compulsory treatment for mental disorder would be permitted in defined circumstances.

Emergency Powers

15. The Committee is recommending a simplification of the existing emergency powers of containment.

The Imposition of Longer Term Compulsion

16. The Committee has endeavoured to recommend a structure which

    i.   will encourage good practice and consensual care,

    ii.   promote public safety,

    iii. provide sufficient independent oversight to protect patients, both those who are able to challenge and those who are not, and

    iv.   does not impose unreasonable demands on professional time and resources.

17. In doing so the Committee has recommended an enhanced role for independent decision making. In a society which now places a high value on the protection of human rights it is essential that decisions which involve significant deprivations of liberty and physical integrity be taken openly and accountably by an independent body.

18. In essence the Committee recommends a structure which would require the care team to apply in writing for a provisional order within seven days of the commencement of compulsory assessment. This order would last for 21 days and would have to be confirmed by an independent reviewer. If the care team wished to extend compulsion beyond 28 days, a compulsory order would have to be confirmed by a full tribunal at an oral hearing. If a patient wished to challenge his or her compulsion in advance of the 28 day tribunal, he or she would have the right to request an expedited tribunal.

The Constitution of the Independent Decision Makers

19. The Committee recommends the creation of a new multi-disciplinary tribunal appointed by the Lord Chancellor. While the Committee appreciates the importance of providing access to medical expertise, it does not wish to retain the practice of the medical member of the tribunal conducting a prior examination of the patient. It describes a number of possible models of tribunal decision making and recommends further consultation on the details.

20.   The Committee recommends that the role of independent reviewer be performed by a legal member of the new tribunal.

The Compulsory Order

21.   The compulsory order would have to be confirmed by the tribunal and could last for any period up to 6 months. The criteria have been devised so as to reflect the Committee's underlying principles and draw a distinction between those patients who lack the capacity to consent to care and treatment for mental disorder and those who retain such capacity. For patients who retain the necessary capacity the grounds for the imposition of compulsion would be significantly more restricted and would relate *primarily* to public safety.

22.   The care team would be required to specify whether the proposed care and treatment was to be provided in hospital or in the community and there would be provision for variation, with the approval of the tribunal, during the course of the order. In the case of an order designed to take effect in the community the order would specify the obligations on all parties. Persistent non-compliance with any condition on the part of the patient which led to a deterioration in his or her mental health would lead to conveyance to and/or re/admission to hospital. Until safe and adequately staffed non-hospital settings are available, medication could only be forcibly administered in a hospital environment.

The Ending of Compulsion

23.   If the entry criteria ceased to be met, the clinical supervisor would be obliged to discharge the patient. Renewals could be confirmed by the tribunal on the application of the clinical supervisor. If the order was to last for more than three months the patient would have the right to apply to the tribunal for discharge once during the course of the order.

24.   The criteria for discharge should reflect the criteria for admission to compulsion and the tribunal should be required to discharge unless satisfied that the criteria for admission continue to be met.

TREATMENT

25.   The Committee recommends that the term treatment be left undefined, but that certain forms of treatment should attract specific safeguards. These treatments include:

- Neurosurgery for mental disorder and other specially invasive treatments;

- Long-term medication;

- Electro Convulsive Therapy ;

- Other controlled treatments, including polypharmacy;

- Feeding contrary to the will of the patient;

- Emergency treatments.

26. The Committee recommends that certain of these safeguards should apply in the case of informal patients as well as in the case of those under a compulsory order.

INCAPACITY

27. The Committee appreciates that the notion of incapacity will require careful definition and recommends a definition in line with that proposed by the Law Commission in its Report *Mental Incapacity*, (Law Commission Cm 231, 1995). The Committee emphasises that there should be a presumption in favour of capacity and that the final decision should rest with the tribunal.

28. Examples are given to illustrate how the definition might be applied in practice and in Chapter 7 the Committee considers some of the more difficult applications of the concept. Whatever the initial difficulties in refining the concept the Committee is convinced that the notion of capacity has an independent value and meaning the core of which is accepted by all those involved in the operation of mental health legislation. The introduction of capacity in place of the current test of 'appropriateness' should lead to a more precise and objectively justifiable use of compulsory powers.

BEST INTERESTS

29. According to the Committee's recommendations approved care and treatment should be in the patient's best interests. The Committee favours a definition of best interests which gives priority to the assumed wishes of the patient as far as they are ascertainable.

COMMON LAW/STATUTE

30. In framing its recommendations the Committee has tried to make the statutory framework as comprehensive as possible, although it still envisages the 'informal' provision of care and treatment for mental disorder in the case of those patients who offer no objection, however expressed. Nonetheless, until there is a statutory framework to cover substitute decision making generally for those people who lack capacity, the Committee considers that treatment for physical disorder must continue to be authorised by the common law where the patient lacks the capacity to consent.

INFORMATION SHARING

31. The Committee is aware that the failure to share information between agencies is frequently referred to in independent homicide inquiries. It recommends that the Code of Practice be expressly required by any new act to provide guidance about the sharing of information in relation to mental health care.

CARERS

32. Throughout the report the Committee emphasises the important role played by carers and the need both to involve them in planning care and treatment and to offer them all necessary support.

SAFEGUARDS

Hospital Managers

33. While paying tribute to the work of hospital managers the Committee considers that under its proposed scheme they would have no proper role. It therefore recommends the removal of the managers' right to discharge.

Second Opinion Appointed Doctors

34. The Committee recommends that the role currently performed by SOADs be transferred to the medical members of the tribunal or to the panel of independent doctors appointed to advise the tribunal.

Training and Approval

35. The Committee makes recommendations for enhancing the scheme for the training, approval and accreditation of those professionals empowered to act under the new legislation.

The Mental Health Act Commission

36. The Committee recommends the continuation of a body such as the MHAC but recommends that it be reconstituted as a body independent of the Secretary of State, reporting directly to Parliament through the select committee structure. Its role should be expanded in a number of respects including an extension of its remit to cover all patients under compulsion, whether in hospital or community settings, and the care and treatment of informal in-patients.

Advance Agreements about Care

37. The Committee is convinced that the creation and recognition of advance agreements about care would greatly assist in the promotion of informal and consensual care. It therefore recommends that an obligation be placed on care teams to provide all patients prior to discharge from compulsion with information about and assistance with the creation of such agreements.

Nearest Relatives and Advocacy

38. The Committee recommends that future legislation make no reference to the nearest relative. Instead the new act should make provision for the identification, by the patient if possible, of a nominated person and should accord that figure certain rights and responsibilities.

39. The Committee is satisfied that access to independent advocacy will be vital if the fundamental principles which underlie its recommendations are to be achieved. The Committee thus recommends

     i.   that a duty be imposed on the Secretary of State to ensure the provision of advocacy,

     ii. that advocates be given specific rights of access to patients under compulsion,

iii   that relevant authorities have a duty to respond to a patient's advocate, and

iv   that a statutory right to advocacy be created at the earliest opportunity.

CHILDREN

40.   The Committee recommends that children continue to be covered by the provisions of mental health legislation. It favours sixteen as the threshold for capacity to make treatment decisions, with a rebuttable presumption of capacity in children from the age of ten or twelve. It further recommends that children subject to compulsion under the new act be entitled to accommodation within an environment which is appropriate to their age.

BOURNEWOOD

41.   The Committee emphasises throughout its report the need to create a statutory framework specifically designed to meet the needs of those who suffer from longterm incapacity, for whatever reason, and thereby to fill the legislative gap revealed by the *Bournewood* case. It is a considerable task which must be addressed with some urgency, not least because the absence of adequate safeguards renders the government vulnerable under the provisions of the ECHR and thus the Human Rights Act.

42.   The Committee makes recommendations concerning the principles which should be reflected within the new framework.

OFFENDERS

43.   The Committee is convinced that a thorough review of Part III of the present Act is essential and recommends that it be conducted in the light of the Committee's own recommendations, before any new legislative provisions are introduced. The Committee identifies issues of principle which, in its view, should underpin any such review and makes certain recommendations concerning the content of future legislation.

44.   The Committee is satisfied that a health disposal must remain available to a sentencing court on the basis of the admission criteria recommended in the context of civil compulsion, but the Committee recommends greater use of interim health orders. The Committee is also satisfied that the power to impose restrictions must be retained but recommends that the power to

grant leave and to authorise transfer between hospitals in the case of restricted patients be extended to the tribunal. The Committee anticipates that the need for conditional discharge will be reduced in the light of the power to apply a compulsory order outside hospital, but it accepts that there will still be a need to retain a mechanism for supervision and ultimate recall to hospital based primarily on considerations of public safety.

PRISONERS

45.   The Committee is convinced that it would be quite inappropriate to permit compulsory treatment for mental disorder in prison. The priority must be to ensure that all those with mental disorder of a severity which would attract compulsion outside prison are transferred to a suitable hospital facility.

46.   The Committee therefore recommends the introduction of a right in prisoners to an assessment of their mental health needs. It further recommends a power in the Secretary of State to direct the transfer of a prisoner to hospital for compulsory assessment. If longterm compulsory care and treatment was required it would then be provided in hospital, under restrictions if necessary, on the authority of the tribunal.

1. INTRODUCTION

Background

1.1. The Committee was established by Ministers in the Department of Health in October 1998. It was asked to give the government advice on how mental health legislation should be shaped to reflect contemporary patterns of care and treatment and to support government policy, as set out in *Modernising Mental Health Services* published in December 1998. The terms of reference are given at Appendix A. The membership of the Committee was set by Ministers to reflect many of the professions contributing to mental health services.

1.2. Our job has not been to make policy but to consider the legislative framework necessary to facilitate the delivery of the government's policies in relation to mental health. In this regard our attention was directed specifically towards the steps that the government is taking to encourage better quality mental health services through the establishment of programmes of national service frameworks and through the provisions contained in the Health Act 1999.

1.3. Our task has been to consider the reforms necessary to make mental health legislation reflect the needs of modern mental health provision. But in setting about this task we have been very conscious of the limit of what can be achieved by law alone. In the first place an appropriate legal framework is only one of a number of components of effective mental health provision: a modern act cannot on its own guarantee an improved level of service. It cannot on its own increase the capacity of the service by creating more beds, crisis centres or trained staff. The creation of a modern legislative framework will not solve the acute lack of services. While we recognise the importance of modernising the law and believe our proposals if implemented would herald a valuable new approach, we must emphasise our firmly held conviction that the introduction of new legal powers will provide no solutions if not backed up by a firm commitment to improve the range and quality of services.

1.4. Secondly, even where its relevance is most direct, the law is likely to have only a limited impact unless it is congruent with the values of those who use it. If the law is to influence the decisions of busy mental health professionals, struggling to provide adequate levels of care with scarce resources, and if it is to address the needs of service users and their carers, it must be seen to reflect the ethics of health care, to encourage rather than to deter good practice and to be practical in the demands it makes. It must also be seen to be fair both in its structure and in its application. The more in tune any new legislation is with the aspirations of those who have to use it, the more it will be followed in practice.

1.5.	Public protection is regarded as an important objective of mental health provision, but a law which fails to command the respect and approval of those who have to implement it will not deliver public safety. In this regard it is important to emphasise that the legislative response to the perceived danger posed by people with a mental disorder must be proportionate to the actual risk. If we are to promote public safety through legislation we must endeavour to do so in a way which attracts the agreement and co-operation of the professionals who will have to work within it.

1.6.	Finally, we are conscious that even the best intentioned legal reform can have unforeseen adverse consequences, and we have been most anxious not to recommend change which might inadvertently undermine aspects of community mental health care which appear to be working well. Thus, although we are satisfied that it is no longer necessary in all cases to deprive a person of liberty in order to ensure the compulsory provision of care and treatment for mental disorder, we wish to avoid extending the scope of compulsion to situations in the community where it is not needed and could be counter-productive. For this reason, we have recommended severing the link between compulsory care and hospital detention in such a way as to avoid increasing the overall use of compulsion.

Our Approach

1.7.	In embarking on our task we decided to regard everything within the 1983 Mental Health Act as susceptible to change. Only in that way did we feel we could provide an adequate review of what might be required in order to construct a legislative framework for mental health care into the next century. *The Key Themes* document which we circulated in November 1998 was devised with that in mind.

1.8.	At the same time we are well aware of the value of retaining structures which are working well and with which users, carers and mental health practitioners are familiar. We have decided therefore to recommend change only where it has been necessary to do so in order to reflect the shape of modern service provision, to meet our European obligations or to satisfy the principles which we consider should govern modern mental health legislation.

1.9.	The way in which we have set about our task is described in Appendix B. Although we have been constrained by the timetable within which we have had to operate, we are satisfied that the programme of consultation and discussion which we have undertaken has been of considerable value and has enabled us to capture the views of a large number of individuals with a wide experience of mental health provision. We would like to express our warm thanks to all those who responded to our requests for help and who offered their views and comments so generously despite the demanding timetable. We understand the difficulties the timing caused for some respondents and we are extremely grateful for the efforts they made to meet the deadlines. We would also like particularly to thank those who submitted specially commissioned papers. They were of immense value in setting out the underlying issues and the context of our task. The majority of the papers are available on the Department of Health's review of the Mental Health Act website: http://193/32.28.83/menhlth.htm

1.10.   In devising our proposals we have been conscious of what we have described above as the limits of the law. We have also been most aware of the need to reflect the demands of modern service provision, to improve public confidence in the system, to strengthen the principle of non-discrimination, to enhance the position of patient autonomy, and at the same time to pursue as simple a structure as is practicable.

1.11.   At the outset we had to address the fundamental question: what is mental health legislation for? The present Mental Health Act is primarily concerned with providing a framework for the compulsory hospitalisation and treatment of certain people with mental disorder. It has little to say about service quality or provision. We had to decide whether to follow this limited model or to recommend a broader focus for the new legislation, one which would address issues of service provision for mental health more generally.

1.12.   On balance we have decided to adopt the first more limited model but to elevate the role of principles within it. We have arrived at this conclusion for the following reasons:

i   We have been assured that questions of service quality are being addressed elsewhere, through the new Health Act, the introduction of clinical governance and the national service frameworks and the initiatives announced in the social services white paper. Like everyone else we have no means of testing this assurance, but we must accept it in the spirit it is given: we are not in a position to recommend the wholesale revision of mental health services.

ii   We are anxious to promote the principle that mental ill health should not form a basis for discrimination. Thus, as far as possible, those suffering from mental disorders should be treated in the same way as those suffering from physical disorders, and wherever practicable, treatment and care for mental disorder should be provided informally, on a consensual basis.

iii Following from this principle of non-discrimination, it is hard to justify the introduction of a legal right to a specific level of mental health care where no equivalent right exists in relation to physical health care. However, notwithstanding the desire for informality, the provision of mental health care, unlike virtually all other forms of health care, may have to be delivered by the use of compulsory powers. In these circumstances we are persuaded that the principle of reciprocity imposes special obligations: when society compels an individual to accept mental health care services those services must be available and of an appropriate quality. We have therefore felt justified in recommending special rights for those who are made subject to compulsion, but at the same time, we have been anxious not to allow that principle to be used to filter resources away from those in need who are not under compulsion.

1.13. Despite taking this narrow approach to our task we would like to make one general recommendation. If we are to move towards a framework for compulsory mental health care in the community then we urge that the opportunity be taken to address, either in the same piece of legislation or at least at the same time, the existing structure of non-compulsory community based services. This would enable simpler transfer between compulsory and voluntary or informal community treatment. We believe that it is now necessary to bring together and consolidate the powers and duties of health and social service authorities, as they relate to the provision of community mental health services, under, for example, the National Assistance Act 1948, the Chronically Sick and Disabled Persons Act 1970, the National Health Service Act 1977, the Disabled Persons (Services, Consultation and Representation) Act 1986, and the National Health Service and Community Care Act 1990.

1.14. In what follows the Committee has tried to identify a framework for future mental health legislation which, in addition to protecting public safety, reflects both the need to provide rights for those subjected to compulsion where appropriate and the need to encourage best practice generally. We are satisfied from the results of our preliminary consultations that the essential framework which we are recommending and the principles which underpin it do reflect the underlying values of those with experience in the field. It is a structure which we believe to be capable of delivering the government's policy objectives in a way which is acceptable to those whose co-operation is vital to their successful achievement. Furthermore, it is a structure with an essential coherence: it must be taken as a whole, few elements of it could survive on their own.

The Need for Further Consultation

1.15. We have already acknowledged that the reform of the Mental Health Act is set within a broader policy context of which we have tried to take account. In addition there have been three specific initiatives within government of particular relevance to the work of the Committee: the introduction of the national service framework, the possibility of proposals emerging from *Who Decides?* (Lord Chancellor's Department 1997, Cm 3803) and the proposals concerning the management of dangerous people with severe personality disorders. Unfortunately none of these initiatives has borne fruit in time for us to take them fully into account.

1.16. Originally we were asked to report in April 1999. This timetable was extended to July 1999 in order to enable us to consult on our Draft Proposals. However, while we are grateful for the extension, the overall timescale, whether 7 months or 10, was always tight and we accepted it on the understanding that our job was to consider the scope of the necessary reforms and the overall structure they might take: further consultation would follow.

1.17. We have now completed our job as best we can. The deadline of 15 July was set for delivery of our report and we have met it. However, we strongly advise that there now be an extended period of consultation: the need is even greater than might have been anticipated at the outset.

1.18 At the time of writing the national service framework has not yet been published, and we have thus been unable to consult on the practicalities of our proposals in the light of the recommended levels of service. It is vital that this is done before any final decisions on legislation are made.

1.19 The anticipated proposals following the publication of *Who Decides?* have not yet materialised. Consequently there has been no opportunity to develop them into a comprehensive framework to provide for the needs of adults with longterm mental incapacity. As we explain throughout the text which follows, this leaves an important gap in the safeguards provided for a significant number of people and one which must be filled as a matter of urgency. Extensive consultation is required in order to shape an appropriate framework.

1.20 The Department of Health and the Home Office have been working on a scheme to provide for those with severe personality disorders who are seen to pose a serious risk to public safety. Again at the time of writing the proposals have not been published. Thus we have been unable to take them fully into account or to consult on them when devising our recommendations with regard to personality disorders within the new legislation as a whole.

1.21 In addition there is the whole question of how the new legislation should deal with those who come to the attention of mental health services through the criminal justice system. Given our timetable and composition we have not felt able either to consult on or to consider adequately this crucial issue. It is our view that the questions raised are highly complex and deserve rigorous consideration but they must be resolved if government is to legislate coherently in this area.

1.22 It has also become apparent to us that the availability of compulsion outside hospital raises fundamental questions about charging policy stretching far beyond the remit of our inquiry. An extensive review of charging policy is required.

1.23 In the course of our work we have become aware of some relevant overseas experience but we have not had the time nor the resources to investigate this potentially valuable source of information. A real attempt should be made to understand the experience of mental health legislation in other jurisdictions so that we may learn from both the successes and the failures before we take any irrevocable steps here.

1.24 We are delighted that the Department of Health has commissioned a programme of research into the workings of the current Mental Health Act, but unfortunately our timetable has not allowed us to reflect the results of this research. In determining its eventual legislative strategy the government must give itself time to take full advantage of these research results.

1.25 Finally, we have already expressed our thanks to all those who have contributed to our deliberations either by responding to our requests for comments or views or by providing commissioned papers. We have been struck by the strength of the views held and by the vigour of the debate. It is our clear impression that there is a rich reserve of knowledge, opinion and expertise which can usefully inform and influence the development and reform of our mental health law. Further consultation is essential if the full value of this combined experience is to be realised.

1.26 The results of our consultations so far have convinced us of the need for fundamental change to the legislative framework for the provision of mental health care. There is a strong body of informed opinion behind the desire for a new modern framework, and we are satisfied that the essential structure which we are recommending in this report represents the correct way forward. However, we urge government to recognise the complexity of the context in which it is proposing to legislate. If it wishes to produce mental health legislation for the twenty-first century which can compare in terms of vision and durability to its real predecessor, the Act of 1959, then both time and extensive consultation are required.

2. GENERAL PRINCIPLES

Underlying Principles

2.1. The desire to encourage the treatment of mental ill health according to principles similar to those which govern the treatment of physical ill health is fundamental to our entire approach. This desire to promote non-discrimination on grounds of mental health has led inevitably to an emphasis on patient autonomy. In the context of physical health a patient with capacity is free to choose whether or not to accept treatment: his or her autonomy is respected.

2.2. In our Draft Proposals we indicated our views on both non-discrimination and patient autonomy, which we defined as meaning 'the freedom to decide for oneself, the ability to make choices which others will respect'. While we received overwhelming support for the principle of patient autonomy many respondents pointed both to the contradiction inherent in the elevation of non-discrimination in a statute which then permits the compulsion of individuals essentially on grounds of mental disorder, and to the failure of our Draft Proposals to maintain a consistent approach to patient autonomy throughout. We recognise the strength of both these comments and therefore think it appropriate to set out the basis of our approach in more detail and the nature of the dilemmas as we see them.

2.3. We are convinced that whatever the precise scope of a mental health act it must primarily be seen as a health measure and must be consistent with the professional ethics of the health services. This is not to deny the importance of public protection but to place it within the appropriate context within which it can best be promoted. The importance of respecting and enhancing patient autonomy is now gaining increased recognition within the health services generally (see for example, *Our Healthier Nation* Department of Health 1999, paras 3.27-3.29 and 3.47-3.50) and we are satisfied that it must acquire similar recognition within mental health services specifically.

2.4. Respect for patient autonomy implies respect for the treatment choices of those who have the capacity necessary to make them. Patient autonomy therefore brings with it an inevitable emphasis on capacity. In the context of mental health this becomes crucially relevant. Many people with a mental disorder will retain the capacity to make treatment decisions but others will not, at points in the course of their disorder they will loose that capacity either temporarily or for a more prolonged period. In order to ensure that people who lack the necessary capacity can none the less receive the care and treatment they require, the law must provide a framework to authorise the application of care and treatment in the absence of their consent, even in the face of their active objection. If the law did not do so it would be preventing their access to treatment.

2.5.   Thus it is clear that one major objective of a mental health act must be to provide such a framework. To do so is congruent with the principles of both non-discrimination and patient autonomy. Indeed not to do so could be said to be discriminatory. That much is widely, if not universally, accepted. The difficulties arise in the case of patients with mental disorder who retain the capacity to make treatment choices and refuse the treatment proposed by clinicians. In the context of physical ill health such capable refusals would prevail, whatever the consequences for the patient. Thus to be faithful to the principle of non-discrimination and consistent in the application of patient autonomy a legislative scheme would have to permit intervention in the absence of consent only in the case of those who lacked capacity: a patient's capable refusal of treatment would have to be allowed to prevail.

2.6.   These points were made by a number of those who responded to our Draft Proposals. For some the issue was clear: a mental health act should authorise treatment in the absence of consent only for those who lack capacity. The refusal to accept treatment by a person with capacity must be respected in the context of mental ill health just as it is in the context of physical ill health, whatever the consequences for the individual. If a person with a mental disorder who refused treatment was thought to pose a serious risk to others then he or she should be dealt with through the criminal justice system, not through a health provision.

2.7.   Those who maintained such a pure approach were in a small minority. There was a much larger body of opinion which was prepared to accept the overriding of a capable refusal in a health provision on grounds of public safety in certain circumstances. The reasons given were in part pragmatic and in part driven by principle. Essentially most of those who commented accepted that the safety of the public must be allowed to outweigh individual autonomy where the risk is sufficiently great and, if the risk is related to the presence of a mental disorder for which a health intervention of likely benefit to the individual is available, then it is appropriate that such intervention should be authorised as part of a health provision. Mental disorder unlike most physical health problems may occasionally have wider consequences for the individual's family and carer, and very occasionally for unconnected members of the public affected by the individual's behaviour, acts and omissions. The Committee supports this reasoning and in what follows we seek to describe a framework which adequately reflects it.

2.8. The issue of harm to self, however, presents a much more intractable dilemma and one on which no consensus has emerged from the responses received. A strict adherence to non-discrimination and patient autonomy would imply that a person's capable refusal must be respected whatever the consequences for him or herself. For many this is an unpalatable conclusion. Equally, however, few if any would wish to return to unchallenged paternalism. The overwhelming support achieved by the principle of patient autonomy indicates that the enforced treatment of the capable and objecting patient simply in the interests of his or her own health as defined by professionals is no longer acceptable.

2.9. The reasons given for rejecting the full implications of patient autonomy, in the case of self harm, while at the same time rejecting unrefined paternalism were again a mixture of principle and pragmatism. They include a belief that the consequences of untreated mental disorder may impact more directly and significantly on carers and relatives than do the consequences of untreated physical disorder, and a disinclination to allow someone with a mental disorder, whether or not they formally retain capacity, to deteriorate beyond a certain point. There is also the practical concern that a failure to allow intervention to protect the patient from serious harm despite his or her capable refusal will lead in practice to the adoption of a very broad interpretation of incapacity.

2.10. Those who would wish to give precedence to autonomy in the case of harm to self argue that, unlike the case of harm to others, there is no countervailing interest at stake which outweighs the principle of respect for autonomy. They also suggest that in the case of most forms of mental disorder the person who is vulnerable to serious harm if untreated is unlikely to retain capacity on any proper understanding of the term and would therefore be treated as lacking capacity. Further they point to clinical experience which suggests that for many disorders of personality, rather than mental illness, treatment under compulsion is likely to be counterproductive.

2.11. As a Committee in receipt of these arguments we are aware they are powerfully held on both sides and are effectively irreconcilable. We believe they reflect a difference in fundamental philosophy which can only be resolved by according preference to one approach over the other. We have set out the alternative views as best we can and invite politicians to make the moral choice between them.

2.12. At various points in the text which follows we have spelt out the consequences which would flow from the choice of one approach over another where those consequences differ according to the approach selected.

2.13. We now return to our specific recommendations with regard to the general principles which should be reflected in any new act.

Principle of Non-Discrimination

2.14. As we have just explained we regard the principle of non-discrimination as central to the provision of treatment and care to those suffering from mental disorder and by non-discrimination in this context we are referring to non-discrimination on grounds of mental health.

2.15. We are aware of the widely held belief that high levels of discrimination currently exist against those with mental disorder and in our Draft Proposals we recommended the introduction of a principle of non-discrimination. For the reasons already given we wish now to endorse that recommendation with minor amendments. Thus we recommend the recognition of the following principle:

- **that wherever possible the principles governing mental health care should be the same as those which govern physical health.**

2.16. However, we accept that it would not be appropriate to express the principle within the act itself. Instead we endorse our earlier recommendations:

i   that the principle be given considerable emphasis within the Code of Practice;

ii   that government be invited to address the issue of non-discrimination in relation to such areas as employment, travel, insurance, housing, education and the public representation of mental disorder.

Express Principles

2.17. Many of the submissions originally received by the Committee stressed the need to articulate general principles to underpin the legislation. The Committee has sympathy with this aim and is anxious to elevate the significance of principle both in the devising of a statutory framework and in its eventual implementation.

2.18. We have already explained the importance we attach to the principle of patient autonomy and the notion of capacity which flows from it. While we have described some of the dilemmas posed by any attempt to adhere with total consistency to its demands, we remain convinced of the importance of patient autonomy as the guiding principle expressed within the act.

2.19. The concept is not new and is currently reflected in the guiding principles contained in the Code of Practice, which states at para 1.1 that people to whom the 1983 Mental Health Act applies should 'be treated and cared for in such a way as to promote to the greatest practicable degree their self determination and personal responsibility, consistent with their own needs and wishes'.

2.20. The Committee considers that any new legislation must be expressly concerned with the recognition and enhancement of patient autonomy. Activities under the legislation should be concerned with preserving or (where possible) restoring autonomy, or (where not possible) protecting those with impaired autonomy. Patient autonomy should only be disregarded in well defined circumstances set out by law.

Other Express Principles

2.21. In our Draft Proposals we listed a number of principles which we wished to see included in any new act as a guide to its implementation. In general these principles attracted strong support and we reproduce them here with some amendments. We do not intend these bald principles to be susceptible to specific enforcement on the part of individuals. Their value as stated at the beginning of the act would be in part rhetorical and educative, but they would also provide a guide as to how the act's provisions should be interpreted. However, since the pursuit of these principles has informed our whole attitude to the substantive details of our recommendations they are reflected throughout the discussion which follows, and in a number of instances should give rise to legal entitlements. The principles which we wish to see included are as follows:

    i   Informal care

           Wherever possible care, treatment and support should be provided without recourse to compulsion.

ii   Least restrictive alternative

Service users should be provided with any necessary care, treatment and support both in the least invasive manner and in the least restrictive manner and environment compatible with the delivery of safe and effective care, taking account of the safety of other patients, carers and staff.

iii   Consensual care

Programmes of care, treatment and support should as far as possible reflect the preferences of the service user, even where intervention in the absence of consent is expressly permitted by law.

iv   Participation

Service users should be fully involved, to the extent permitted by their individual capacity, in all aspects of their assessment, care, treatment and support.

v   Reciprocity

Where society imposes an obligation on an individual to comply with a programme of treatment and care it should impose a parallel obligation on the health and social care authorities to provide appropriate services, including ongoing care following discharge from compulsion.

vi   Respect for diversity

Service users should receive care, treatment and support in a manner that accords respect for their individual qualities, abilities and diverse backgrounds, and properly takes into account their age, gender, sexual orientation, ethnic group and social, cultural and religious background.

vii   Equality

All powers under the act, particularly those relating to access to services, assessments and the provision of services shall be exercised without any direct or indirect discrimination on the grounds of physical disability, age, gender, sexual orientation, race, colour, language, religion, or national, ethnic or social origin.

viii   Carers

Those who provide care to service users on an informal basis should receive respect for their role and experience and have their views and needs taken into account.

ix   Effective communication

Service users are entitled to the benefit of the effective sharing of information, consistent with the obligations of confidentiality and the law, amongst those responsible for their care and treatment.

x   Provision of information

Service users should be provided with all the information necessary to enable them to participate fully in the sense envisaged in principle 2.21.iv. (All such information must be provided in a way which renders it most likely to be understood and also in writing where appropriate).

2.22. The Committee is aware of omitting from the above list some of the general principles advocated in the submissions and in the responses to the Draft Proposals. In some cases, particularly with regard to those principles concerned with the processes of formal decision making, the Committee has considered it unnecessary to express them as distinct principles, preferring rather to reflect them where appropriate in the nature of its main recommendations.

2.23. Finally, in our Draft Proposals we sought views on whether we should include a principle of 'evidence based medicine' or 'effective treatment', and if so how such a principle might be expressed. We received a number of helpful comments from which we draw the following points. The principle:

i   should refer to evidence based practice rather than medicine to indicate that it covers the full range of therapeutic interventions;

ii   should make reference to basing interventions on the best research evidence available at the time;

iii   should take account of the views of service users as to the benefits to be received from the intervention.

2.24. We conclude that there is considerable support for including such a principle but that it will require very careful drafting.

2.25. It is our firm view that a mental health act which respects and implements these principles will be more effective in promoting the protection of the public. As we explained in our **Introduction**, legislation is most effective when it reflects the values and ethics of those concerned with its implementation and thereby attracts their agreement and co-operation.

Monitoring the Act

2.26. The Committee is satisfied that the current system has failed to collect adequate data on the operation of the 1983 Act. It regards this as a significant failing, particularly in light of the fact that the Act authorises the deprivation of liberty and the administration of compulsory treatment. In the Draft Proposals we expressed our intention to recommend that a duty be imposed on the Secretary of State to provide for the collection of certain data. Again this recommendation met with widespread support and a number of respondents mentioned specific aspects of the operation of the current Act which they felt called for urgent monitoring. We therefore endorse our original recommendation that the Secretary of State be obliged to provide for the collection of:

i   systematic data on the operation of the new act;

ii   the data necessary to measure the implementation of the principles.

2.27. In addition we recommend that there be an obligation to publish such data annually and that further consultation be undertaken to establish how best to collect, analyse and present the necessary data.

The Code of Practice

2.28. The Committee is convinced that the Code of Practice plays an extremely valuable role in guiding good practice. In our Draft Proposals we explained that although we were keen to enhance this role, we were, on balance, against recommending that the Code be given statutory force. We expressed the view that the need to retain flexibility and the ability to update and amend suggest that its present legal status as official guidance is to be preferred. However, a number of those who responded urged otherwise and wanted to see the Code given statutory force. It was argued that other codes, such as that published under the authority of the Police and Criminal Evidence Act, have statutory force and are still amended as frequently as the Mental Health Act Code.

2.29. While we accept the force of this point we remain convinced that if the Code of Practice were to be given statutory force it would take on a very different form. In particular it would be less able to promote good practice in addition to dealing with details of the implementation of the act itself. We therefore repeat our initial recommendation that the Code be not given statutory force. However, the possibility that the Code be included within the remit of clinical governance and that knowledge of and compliance with the Code be contained within individual employment contracts met with considerable support. We therefore endorse our recommendation that other ways of enhancing the authority of the Code be explored.

2.30. Further, because we are recommending an enhanced role for the Code, we are anxious to ensure that its requirements attract the widest possible respect and acceptance. To this end we recommend that the consultation requirements imposed on the Secretary of State in the new act be made more specific. And finally, as a way of emphasising the Code's significance, we recommend that the statutory authority for the Code appear towards the beginning of the act, immediately following the statement of general principles, and be accompanied by an express presumption of compliance.

3. ENTITLEMENTS

Introduction

3.1. The Committee has been told that initiatives are underway within the Department of Health and the National Health Service to create a framework for the provision of safe, sound and supportive mental health services. Thus, as we have explained above, we do not consider it appropriate to address general questions of service provision within an act which must primarily be concerned with the application of compulsion; although we have recommended that thought be given to the rationalisation of the statutory framework governing the provision of community mental health services.

Consequences of the Principle of Reciprocity

3.2. Whatever the position as regards the provision of services generally, however, we are agreed that the principle of reciprocity demands the provision of extra assurance in the case of those on whom society imposes compulsion. If society is to impose a duty to comply with treatment and care on some of those who suffer from mental disorder it must impose a parallel duty on health and social care authorities to provide an appropriate standard of treatment and care.

3.3. As we explained in our Draft Proposals, however, we are aware that if this simple, and in our view, incontrovertible principle were to be implemented on its own there would be an immediate danger of distortion to the pattern of service provision. Resources might be filtered away from informal care, which in turn would conflict with the desire to favour informal care over compulsion, as set out in principle 2.21.i. above.

3.4. It may be that the obligations imposed by the Health Act 1999 together with the requirements of the national service frameworks combined with clinical governance will be sufficient to deliver high levels of service to all categories of user. But at this early stage it is hard for us to judge the practical impact of these new initiatives. In particular we have had no opportunity to study and to consult upon the substance of the national service framework. We thus consider it necessary to give some thought to the additional mechanisms which might be required in order to guard against any distortion in service provision.

3.5. The possibilities which we listed in our Draft Proposals were as follows:

    i   specific reference in the national service frameworks to the need to achieve the same quality of service irrespective of the user's legal status;

ii   specific reference within the duties of the Commission for Care Standards;

iii   inclusion within the requirements of clinical governance;

iv   clear guidance in the Code of Practice;

v   the introduction of a duty on the Secretary of State to monitor the quality of care provided as between those placed under compulsion and those in receipt of care informally.

3.6. The response to these proposals has been very positive, with many respondents advocating a combination of all five suggestions. There is a very strong desire to see the provision of adequate levels of care generally in order to avoid crises and to support the provision of informal care wherever possible. We therefore recommend the above for serious consideration.

Rights which Flow from Compulsion

3.7. In addition to the general obligation to provide services which flows from the principle of reciprocity, we recommend the introduction of a number of specific rights with corresponding duties which would apply to patients under compulsion, whether detained in hospital or not. These rights, which reflect the principles listed above at para 2.21, should include:

i   the right to information about treatment and care;

ii   at the earliest possible opportunity, the right to advocacy (this is discussed further below at paras 12.24-27);

iii   the right of access to medical records (see Access to Health Records Act 1990) and the right to enter reservations as to the accuracy of factual statements contained therein;

iv   the right to receive care and treatment in accordance with the care plan during any period of compulsion;

v   the right to ongoing care after any period of compulsion;

vi   in the case of those detained in hospital, the right to safe containment consistent with respect for human dignity;

vii   the right to information about and assistance with drawing up an advance agreement.

3.8.   The rights described at 3.7.iv. and 3.7.v. are implied by the principle of reciprocity and attracted very strong support in the responses received to the Draft Proposals. We consider it to be essential to the acceptability of the imposition of compulsion that all patients who are subjected to compulsory powers should gain the right to care and treatment in accordance with the care plan. In effect there would be a right to receive the care and treatment approved by the tribunal (see below). It is also our view that the obligations flowing from reciprocity do not end immediately on discharge from compulsion. A person who has been subject to a period of compulsion would have a right to ongoing care for a specified period after compulsion, although there would be no obligation in the patient to accept that care. The right described at 3.7.v. would replace the current section 117.

3.9.   The rights at 3.7.iv. and 3.7.v. would be personal rights in the compelled patient and would impose duties on health and social service authorities in addition to any general duties they might possess. We would expect enforcement in the first instance to be via established complaints procedures.

3.10.   In relation to para 3.7.v. we appreciate that there are difficulties in identifying the moment at which the right to ongoing care should cease. In our Draft Proposals we suggested that the ongoing care plan approved by the tribunal should specify a period during which the patient would have a right to ongoing care if he or she wished to accept it (for compulsory care and treatment outside hospital see below Chapter 5). At the end of that period the patient's priority access to mental health services would cease. Although there was support for this proposal there were those who felt that the issue of duration might be better addressed within the Code of Practice. On balance, however, we consider that if the ongoing care package is to give rise to an individual right in the patient it is preferable for its duration to be known from the outset. We therefore recommend that the tribunal be asked to determine the matter and the clinical team be given the power to seek an extension if appropriate, or to request a formal early termination if the patient indicates a consistent desire to distance him or herself from care.

3.11.   The question of charging for social care services provided either to a person subject to a compulsory order in the community, or to a person on discharge from compulsion, under para 3.7.v. above, was considered in the

Draft Proposals. Relatively few respondents addressed the topic and of those who did several were against charging altogether. The majority of those who responded were against charging for services delivered under a compulsory order.

3.12. The difficulties encountered in any attempt to resolve the question of charging are compounded by the following:

i   the existing uncertainties about the application of section 117 of the current Act;

ii   the apparent anomaly that social services can be charged for whereas health services are free;

iii   the inconsistency in charging policies between local authorities in the absence of a national charging policy;

iv   the need to ensure the compatibility of any new charging scheme with both other charging regimes and the benefits structure;

v   the need to guard against the creation of perverse incentives;

vi   the need to avoid the appearance of the level of service being determined by the legal status of the patient.

3.13. In relation to charging for social care services provided as part of a compulsory order we now outline three possible options, but in the light of the wider implications flowing from the choice we express no preference between them. The three options are:

i.   Charging for all services
       No distinction is made between a person subject to compulsion and a person receiving services informally. This presents a dilemma in that it requires someone to accept certain services against his or her will and then insists that the individual pay for them.

ii.   Charging for some services
       Services provided under a compulsory order are provided free, except in the case of services for which the patient would pay in the normal course of events. Thus if a patient was required to reside at his or her normal address the expectation would be that he or she would meet the costs of that accommodation in the normal way. If the required residence is in supported accommodation, care costs

would be met by the relevant authority and the patient would be expected to meet normal living expenses like food, utilities and rent, provided the individual had no pre-existing financial commitment to other accommodation.

iii. All services are free

This option, while attractively simple, presents a real danger of perverse incentives: patients may 'choose' to remain subject to compulsion in order to avoid paying for services. Further, if normal living expenses cannot be charged for there would have to be some transfer of resources to local authorities since these expenses are currently met centrally through the benefits system.

3.14. In relation to charging for ongoing services in the period immediately following compulsion the arguments are slightly different. Patients in receipt of services following a period of compulsion are not obliged to accept those services, thus the case for their provision free of charge is arguably less strong than it is in relation to a compulsory order. On the other hand, while such patients are not being compelled to receive the specified services we have argued that the principle of reciprocity entitles them to a certain priority: they are entitled to receive the services for the period specified. Some would argue that this principle of reciprocity extends beyond the mere provision of a service to include its provision free of charge. According to such an argument there should be no distinction in the charging scheme for those under a compulsory order and those in receipt of ongoing care for a specified period following compulsion. If any such distinction were created there would again be a danger of perverse incentives: patients might refuse to accept ongoing care voluntarily in order to attract a community order with the ensuing financial benefits.

3.15. As we suggested in the **Introduction** we regard the whole question of charging for services provided outside hospital as immensely complex, even under the existing structure. If compulsion under mental health legislation is to be extended beyond hospital for civil patients the issue will become yet more complicated. We recommend that a comprehensive review of charging policy be undertaken.

Access to Services

A User's Right to an Assessment of Mental Health Needs

3.16. From the submissions we received in response to Key Themes we became aware of considerable concern about the difficulties which can be encountered in gaining access to the necessary specialist mental health services. This concern was expressed by users, carers, mental health practitioners and the police. In our Draft Proposals we therefore recommended the introduction of a right to assessment and this attracted widespread support. There were, however, questions posed generally concerning the identification of the responsible service and specifically concerning the role of primary care, and reservations expressed concerning the effect of such a right if it did not involve a right to have assessed needs met.

3.17. In our Draft we suggested that the proposed right to assessment would supplement any rights contained elsewhere, section 47 of the NHS and Community Care Act 1990 for example. It would be a right to assessment in relation to mental health needs. It would apply to those in contact with services who might, for example, believe that their condition is deteriorating, and to those unknown to services who believe that they need an assessment in the interests of their own mental health, own safety or for the protection of others. The right would reside in the user or potential user and would impose a duty on the relevant health or social service authority. It could be used as a trigger to the formal process of assessment described below in Chapter 5. We did not envisage the right as a personal right enforceable by the user in private law, but rather as a right giving rise to a public law duty on the relevant authority.

3.18. By the introduction of such a right we are trying to ensure that an individual's mental health needs are taken seriously when they ask for help. We are aware of a recent survey which suggests that one in three people with a severe mental illness are turned away when seeking help (*Better Act Now* National Schizophrenia Fellowship 1999). Our proposal is designed to help remedy this serious gap.

3.19. We would envisage that the primary referral route would be by way of the G.P. whether in relation to a person known to specialist services or not. The significant contribution made by primary care services to mental health care should be recognised. G.P.s should be encouraged to engage with specialist mental health services and to request the assessment of a patient by such services. They should also expect to be appropriately involved in the process of assessment and subsequent care. There is a need for effective communication between the primary health care team and the involved specialist agencies to ensure that service users obtain consistent information and treatment.

3.20. In addition there will be occasions when those known to services approach the relevant mental health team directly and they should also expect assessment. Finally there will be those who present to an Accident and Emergency Department and a suitable referral system should be in place there as well.

3.21. The right as proposed would be to an assessment of mental health needs. The individual should be entitled to have those needs assessed by an appropriately trained professional and to be told the outcome. The precise details of how the scheme would work would have to be supplied in the Code of Practice, and would have to include a system for recording any unmet assessed needs and the provision of guidance as to how to deal with those who in effect abuse the right.

A Carer's Right to Request an Assessment of Mental Health Needs

3.22. In our Draft Proposals we sought views on the extension of the right to assessment to others who might feel the need to have a friend or family member assessed. In the responses there was widespread support for a legal right in carers to ask for the mental health needs of a relevant service user to be assessed, to have their request taken seriously and to be given written reasons if it is decided not to undertake such an assessment. We therefore recommend the introduction of such a right and would suggest that 'carer' in this context be defined so as to include:

i   the nominated person, if such exists (see below paras 12.16-12.23);

ii   any person who provides a substantial amount of care on a regular basis;

iii   any other person with a significant interest in the welfare of the person to be assessed.

3.23. Again, as above, it would be necessary for the Code of Practice to supply the details of how the scheme might work.

A Police 'Right' to Request an Assessment

3.24. For the obligation on local social service and health authorities to respond to police requests for assessment, see below, para 15.27.

Right to Asylum

3.25. In our Draft Proposals we considered the possibility of making provision for those suffering from a mental disorder, possibly very small in number, who volunteer themselves for secure containment in the interests of their own safety or that of others. We indicated that we would like to encourage the provision of secure 'asylum' in such cases and would recommend that the price users would pay for entry to such provision would be a binding undertaking that should they subsequently withdraw consent they would automatically be channelled through the formal assessment process as described below.

3.26. This proposal received both support and opposition. We have given careful consideration to all the responses and since the disadvantages appear to outweigh the benefits we have decided against recommending that such a right to asylum be introduced. There will, in any event, be a right to an assessment of mental health needs, as described above.

The Protection of Remaining Civil Liberties

3.27. Throughout all our proposals outlined below we have sought to ensure that any deprivation of liberty suffered by a patient is:

   i   kept to the minimum possible consistent with safe and effective care;

   ii   subject to review by an independent body where ever practicable.

3.28. This section concentrates on the need to ensure that those who are made subject to compulsion nonetheless retain all those rights and liberties which are not of necessity removed by the fact of compulsion. While it focuses mainly on the position of patients who are detained in hospital, it is important to emphasise that the principle is the same whether or not the compulsion involves detention. If, and in so far as, anti-discrimination legislation such as the Race Relations Act 1976 and the Sex Discrimination Act 1975 does not extend to persons subject to the exercise of compulsory powers, we recommend that such protection should be so extended.

3.29. The detained patient suffers additional deprivation of rights through the fact of detention and we thus regard it as essential to provide special protection for the remaining rights of those patients. The following proposals are designed to ensure that no further deprivation of liberty is imposed on the detained patient save that which is either expressly authorised by the legislation or is necessarily implied by the need to achieve safe containment.

3.30. To a large extent many of the issues revolve around the question of control and discipline. The law as it stands is in need of clarification as the 1983 Act gives little guidance to either patients or clinicians. We received very helpful submissions on this issue initially and the response to our Draft Proposals has been most positive. We are persuaded of the need to provide more statutory guidance, possibly by way of Statutory Instrument supplemented by the Code of Practice. Such guidance would:

i   cover the use of seclusion, other forms of solitary confinement and all forms of restraint;

but would extend also to regulate:

ii   the administration of emergency medication for the protection of others;

iii   powers to search patients;

iv   powers to withhold property;

v   powers to refuse access to areas of the hospital or to hospital activities;

vi   powers to interfere with a patient's freedom to communicate or associate with others.

3.31. The statutory guidance, which would have to pay particular regard to our obligations under the Human Rights Act and thus the European Convention on Human Rights (ECHR), would indicate the grounds on which such powers could be used and the procedures necessary to ensure the proper application of the powers. It would also provide for a means of appeal for the patient through the normal complaints procedures in the first instance.

3.32. In addition it is important to emphasise the issue of patient safety. In para 3.7 we recommended the recognition of a patient's right to safe containment consistent with respect for human dignity. Detained patients cannot choose with whom they are detained and must be offered all reasonable protection from assault (see also below, para 12.30). For example, patients should have a choice of accommodation in safe single sex wards.

3.33. Finally, the Committee is aware of the necessity to guard against possible implications of the introduction of a capacity test when it comes to establishing an individual's civil rights. It will be essential to indicate that the capacity which is being judged for the purposes of mental health legislation is the capacity to decide whether or not to accept care and treatment for mental disorder. A finding of incapacity on that issue should not be allowed to dictate the approach taken to the person's capacity with regard to, for example, the right to marry, to enter into a contract or to vote.

Duty to Establish Local Arrangements

3.34. The current Code of Practice emphasises the importance of inter-agency co-operation (para 2.43). In our Draft Proposals we expressed the view that such co-operation is essential to the proper delivery of mental health services and described our intention to recommend that a duty to work together be imposed on all agencies with responsibilities under the act.

3.35. Again this suggestion attracted considerable support although there was no agreement as to the preferred model. We therefore recommend that a statutory obligation to work together be introduced and that further consultation be conducted in order to determine the appropriate model to be adopted.

4. THE SCOPE OF COMPULSION

Introduction

4.1. For the reasons we have given above we have taken the view that the primary purpose of any new mental health legislation should be to provide a framework for the appropriate exercise of compulsory powers. However, in this context the notion of compulsion needs some further explanation. We have argued that where a patient lacks the capacity to consent to care and treatment for mental disorder then society should have the power to provide that care and treatment even in the absence of the person's consent. Thus the primary function of the proposed structure is to enable mental health services to care appropriately for those who are unable to authorise that care and treatment themselves: it is 'compulsory' essentially because it empowers mental health professionals to intervene in the absence of consent, whether passively or actively displayed.

4.2. There is, of course, a further sense in which the structure is compulsory. In certain circumstances society is also justified in intervening in the face of a clear refusal to consent to treatment for mental disorder on the part of a person with the capacity to make that choice. As we have explained above, the precise extent of the circumstances in which such a denial of an individual's autonomy is felt to be justified within a health statute is ultimately a matter of moral judgment.

4.3. The question of how to define those who should come within the scope of the compulsory framework must be considered against this background. In what follows we describe our preferred approach: a broad primary diagnostic criterion with some express exclusions, coupled to rigorous entry criteria, the strictness of which increases as the patient progresses from assessment to a compulsory order.

The Diagnostic Criterion

4.4. As we described in our Draft Proposals we received a number of initial submissions in response to our Key Themes document which addressed the question of the diagnostic trigger for compulsion. Of those the vast majority were in favour of a redefinition of mental disorder. There was, however, no agreement as to the preferred definition. In short there was a tension between a definition which was so broad it was open to abuse and one that was too narrow and risked missing people who might benefit from the provisions of the act or on whom the provisions of the act should be applied for the protection of others. There was also felt to be a danger of entrenching in legislation a definition which might quickly become outdated as clinical practice develops.

4.5. On balance we favoured a broad definition of the basic diagnostic criterion and in our Draft Proposals we recommended simply retaining the term 'mental disorder' which we suggested might be defined according to the Law Commission's proposed definition as 'any disability or disorder of mind or brain, whether permanent or temporary, which results in an impairment or disturbance of mental functioning' (*Mental Incapacity*, paras 3.8 - 3.13). We appreciated that the Law Commission, which was making recommendations with regard to incapacity, was anxious to establish a definition which was not restricted to psychiatric disorder but we felt that the definition could apply with equal merit in a mental health act.

4.6. In our Draft Proposals we also recommended that definitional schemes such as the International Classification of Disease (ICD-10) and the Diagnostic and Statistical Manual (DSM IV) be referred to in the Code of Practice as a guide.

4.7. A large majority of those who responded on these issues supported the broad definition although there were some who felt it was too wide. In some cases this concern was related to the broad criteria for compulsory assessment which we were then proposing and we would hope that such concerns will have been answered by the revisions to the criteria which we have suggested below. Others suggested specific amendments and in particular our attention was drawn to the definition proposed by the Scottish Law Commission (1995) which includes more express exclusions than we initially recommended.

4.8. In the light of these responses we are satisfied that mental disorder should be used as the primary diagnostic criterion and that the Code of Practice should refer to the suggested definitional schemes, including the World Health Organisation's International Classification of Impairments Disabilities and Handicaps (WHO 1980, but currently under revision). As to the definition of mental disorder itself we still favour the Law Commission's definition but consider that it would be valuable to consult further with Scottish colleagues who are currently working up proposals for reform. The adoption of the same definition both sides of the border would seem desirable.

Exclusions

4.9. In our Draft Proposals we suggested that the specific exclusions contained within the 1983 Act were no longer necessary, although we recommended that disorders of sexual preference should be excluded as sufficient on their own to constitute mental disorder, particularly if reference is made to ICD-

10. We now endorse that recommendation with regard to disorders of sexual preference.

4.10. In our Key Themes document we asked for views on the inclusion or otherwise of a wide range of specific categories of people. With regard to substance misuse the prevailing view amongst those who commented was that although substance misuse on its own should not be regarded as a mental disorder, the prevalence of co-morbidity suggests it should be possible to use the powers of the act to assess someone who was presenting as possibly mentally disordered as well as being under the influence of drugs or alcohol. In order to ensure that such people were not simply turned away, we recommended in our Draft Proposals that the existing exclusion of 'dependence on alcohol or drugs' as the sole grounds for mental disorder be abandoned. We expressed the view that if it eventually transpired after assessment that the person had no underlying mental disorder s/he would never meet the entry criteria for compulsion and would be discharged.

4.11. The response to this recommendation has been mixed. It would appear that all those professionals who responded were keen to ensure that co-morbidity is adequately treated. Some liked the recommendations because they felt that they would achieve this end, while others feared that the removal of the exclusion would lead to counterproductive compulsion being imposed on substance misuse alone. On balance we accept the latter argument and would now recommend that drug and alcohol misuse should be excluded as a **sole** ground for believing mental disorder to be present. However, we are very aware of the relationship between substance misuse and violence illustrated most recently in the context of homicide by the National Confidential Inquiry's Report *Safer_Services* (Department of Health 1999) and the prevalence of co-morbidity. Therefore in terms of public safety we consider it essential that both the Code of Practice and the relevant professional training emphasise the complex relationships between substance misuse, mental disorder and violence.

Personality Disorders

4.12. There was almost universal agreement among those who commented, both on Key Themes and in response to our Draft Proposals, that the term 'psychopathic disorder' be removed from the Act. This was also the view of the *Report of the Committee of Inquiry into the Personality Disorder Unit, Ashworth Special Hospital* (HMSO Cm 4194-11, 1999). The Committee so recommends.

4.13. On the inclusion of personality disorder opinion in response to Key Themes was divided. For those who favoured exclusion the essential argument was that, although personality disorders might be classified as mental disorders (see ICD-10), they were not treatable and should not therefore be subjected to compulsion under mental health legislation. In our Draft Proposals we acknowledged this argument, but we expressed reluctance to see personality disorders as such excluded from the provisions of any new act entirely for the following reasons:

i   the co-occurrence of personality disorders and mental illness would make exclusion difficult;

ii   within the variety of conditions covered by the term personality disorder are those such as borderline personality disorders, which may be more susceptible to therapeutic intervention than others;

iii   although personality disorders may not be susceptible to drug therapy, the Committee is concerned that their removal from the act would serve to set back even further the development of sustained research into alternative methods of treatment.

4.14. This reasoning attracted broad support. Personality disorders would certainly be included within the basic diagnostic criterion, mental disorder, and for the avoidance of doubt we proceed on the basis that they also fall within the broad definition of mental disorder which we are now recommending. We endorse the recommendation in our Draft Proposals that personality disorders should not be expressly excluded from the new act.

4.15. However, while personality disorders will fall within the broad criterion for assessment it is likely that in a number of cases the condition will fail to meet the strict criteria necessary for the imposition of a compulsory order after assessment. In particular many of those with personality disorders may be found to have the necessary capacity to choose for themselves whether to accept care and treatment. In such cases, unless there is another interest deemed to override the need to respect their autonomy (see below for the precise criteria), compulsory powers would not be applicable.

4.16. Evidence suggests that the incidence of personality disorders is particularly high within the prison population (*Psychiatric Morbidity among Prisoners*, Government Statistical Service 1998) and we would certainly wish to retain the possibility of a hospital disposal where appropriate in cases where the offender is suffering from a personality disorder but does not present the level of risk which may be required to attract the special scheme to be provided for those with severe personality disorders.

Learning Disability, Dementia, Acquired Brain Disorders and other similar Enduring Disabilities

4.17. As we have already explained, the problems raised by the need to find an appropriate framework for the provision of treatment and care to those with learning disabilities have been among the most difficult faced by the Committee. In part this is due to the need to fill the legislative gap revealed by the *Bournewood* decision ([1998] 3 W.L.R. 107) and the absence of formal proposals from the Lord Chancellor's Department following on from the publication of *Who Decides?*

4.18. It is imperative that an appropriate statutory framework of substitute decision making and safeguards be created to provide the necessary care and support to those who lack capacity in the long term through, for example, severe learning disability. We appreciate that learning disability is not unique in this respect and the substance of what we say below may apply equally to other forms of mental disorder such as dementia, acquired brain injury and some forms of pervasive developmental disorder.

4.19. We have received clear submissions, on behalf of both those with learning disabilities and those who care for them, to the effect that a mental health act is not the appropriate vehicle for the provision of such a framework. The principal reasons given include:

  i   the care and support required in the case of learning disability extends much further than treatment for mental disorder;

  ii   people with a learning disability do not, on the whole, require medical treatment for mental disorder;

  iii   inclusion within a mental health act is thought to be stigmatising for the patient and for the family;

  iv   the need for care and support in the case of learning disability is typically long standing, while for mental illness needs may fluctuate;

  v   the formal structure required for the imposition of compulsion in the case of mental disorder would not be appropriate to learning disability.

4.20. While we appreciate the strength of this reasoning and fully support the argument that a new comprehensive statutory framework is required, we nonetheless do not wish to see learning disabilities expressly excluded from any new mental health act. In the first place we consider it important to ensure that assessment, under compulsion if necessary, is available for those with a learning disability and a co-occurring mental illness. Secondly, there may be those with a learning disability who display challenging behaviour, including self harm, for whom care and treatment under the framework provided by a mental health act would be appropriate. These views attracted wide support in the responses to our Draft Proposals and we do not therefore recommend that learning disability be expressly excluded from the diagnostic criterion.

4.21. However, it is important to appreciate that if learning disabilities remain within the act then those with learning disabilities who do require care and treatment for their mental disorder could be eligible to receive a compulsory order if all the other criteria are fulfilled. At the time of our Draft Proposals we had hoped that legislative proposals would emerge from *Who Decides?* which could be used to provide a framework specifically designed to meet the needs of people with learning disabilities comprehensively, not just in relation to treatment for mental disorder. In which case we anticipated that a person with a learning disability who came into contact with the formal mental health structure would be diverted as soon as possible to that more comprehensive framework.

4.22. Unfortunately we now realise that no legislative proposals from *Who Decides?* will emerge in the near future. We are therefore left with the possibility that there may be people with learning disabilitiy and longterm incapacity who the law may regard as being detained, albeit under common law not the mental health act, and for whom no proper safeguards exist. In these circumstances such people may have to enter into longterm compulsory care and treatment under the new mental health legislation in order to acquire the required safeguards, even if they have a learning disability alone and no mental illness. Until a comprehensive statutory framework dealing with longterm incapacity is provided, mental health legislation will be the only mechanism available. We do not regard such an outcome as either desirable or appropriate. For the reasons stated above we do not think people who require care and treatment for their learning disabilities should be provided for under a mental health act designed primarily for those with other forms of mental disorder.

4.23. However, for the reasons given above, we wish in the longterm to retain learning disability within the scope of the new act in order to provide for the assessment of co-morbidity and the care and treatment of challenging behaviours. We are most reluctant to compromise this longterm objective merely to guard against possible difficulties arising from the current lack of a comprehensive framework for longterm incapacity.

4.24. Instead we repeat our conviction that a comprehensive statutory framework to meet the needs of those who lack capacity on a longterm basis must be provided as a matter of urgency, not least in order to meet our obligations under the Human Rights Act. Such a framework would cover people with learning disabilities, but certainly would not be limited to them. We are strongly of the view that merely to provide a framework for treatment and care for mental disorder by way of a mental health act would be inadequate and unwise. The problem stretches far beyond the proper confines of a mental health act and deserves its own consideration. Much of the work has already been done by the Law Commission and the Lord Chancellor's Department in *Who Decides?* This work needs now to be developed in the light of the *Bournewood* decision and the likely implications of the Human Rights Act.

4.25. We have referred here and earlier to the need for a **statutory** framework. Although duties are imposed and rights protected currently under the common law, it is our firm view that the imposition of a comprehensive scheme of substitute decision making for adult incapacitated citizens, which creates new rights and imposes new obligations, can only be achieved by act of Parliament. This is not an objective which, lawfully and consistently with ECHR requirements, can be achieved by government directions or guidance. The courts retain neither an inherent, nor a parens patriae, jurisdiction to deal with these problems.

4.26. We offer below, para 14.3, some brief recommendations relating to the principles which should be reflected within the new statutory framework. The tight timetable and the uncertain legislative landscape within which we have been working have made it impossible for us to do more.

5. THE STRUCTURE OF COMPULSORY POWERS

Introduction

5.1. In thinking about the shape of the formal structure for the application of compulsion we have tried to devise as simple and as flexible a model as possible and one which empowers mental health professionals to take the necessary action as swiftly and as sensitively as is compatible with safe and effective care. We have also been conscious of the changing configuration of services and the shift in emphasis away from primarily hospital based care. At the same time we have been determined to include sufficient safeguards to ensure appropriate protection of the patient's individual dignity, autonomy and human rights. To this end we are recommending the automatic introduction of an independent decision maker at certain crucial stages in the process of compulsion. We have also been anxious to support our desire to encourage consensual care. Thus we have emphasised the importance of the provision of full information to patients, the availability of independent advocacy to support both patients and carers and, wherever possible, the use of advance agreements.

An Outline of the Proposed Process

5.2. **Assessment**

    i   In cases where attempts to engage informal care have failed compulsory assessment must be available;

    ii   Entry to assessment would be on the recommendation of three professionals;

    iii   The formal detainer/compeller would be the trust, or in relation to the independent healthcare sector, the person or persons registered under the Registered Homes Act 1984;

    iv   Compulsory assessment would be in hospital including any properly registered independent psychiatric hospital or mental nursing home, formal assessment could be conducted in the community;

    v   Compulsion would last for a maximum of 7 days, compulsory treatment would be available in certain circumstances;

    vi   Specific tasks would be given to the care team.

5.3. **Independent decision maker - for the patient who takes no positive steps to challenge**

    i   On day 7 compulsion will end unless the care team applies on paper to the independent reviewer to confirm a provisional 21 day order;

    ii   The independent reviewer may;

        (a)   confirm a 21 day order;

        (b)   call for more information;

        (c)   call for an expedited tribunal.

    iii   During the 21 days the care team has the power/obligation to discharge the patient from compulsion if the statutory criteria are no longer met;

    iv   At day 28 all compulsion will end unless the tribunal has confirmed the care team's application for a compulsory order, maximum duration 6 months.

5.4. **Independent decision maker - for the patient who wishes to challenge his/her compulsion**

    i   Between day 1 and day 14 the patient has the right to request an expedited tribunal;

    ii   Confirmation of the provisional order by the independent reviewer would still be required at day 7, the reviewer may discharge the patient;

    iii   An expedited tribunal must meet within 7 days of patient's request;

    iv   The expedited tribunal would have similar powers to those possessed by a tribunal at 28 days.

Assessment

5.5. We have already described our recommendations in relation to a right to assessment of mental health needs. This right we regard as an essential consequence of the desire to encourage informal care which was shared by virtually all our respondents. We now turn to consider those cases where, for whatever reason, the provision of informal care and treatment has failed.

5.6. For those deemed to require an assessment of their mental health needs but who either do not co-operate or lack the capacity to do so the Committee favours retaining a compulsory assessment power. Authority to impose compulsory assessment would remain as at present in the hands of mental health professionals. In its Draft Proposals the Committee indicated that it wished to recommend a shorter compulsory assessment period than the current 28 days and the introduction of more rigorous assessment requirements during that shorter period. While many respondents expressed reservations concerning aspects of the initial proposals the essential notion of a shorter more rigorous assessment process attracted considerable support. Thus, taking into account the helpful comments we have received, we would now make the following broad recommendations.

Mental Health Act Assessment

5.7. At present a formal mental health act assessment requires the participation of the applicant, who is typically an ASW but can be the nearest relative, and two medical practitioners. Requirements concerning independence, expertise and, where practicable, previous knowledge of the patient are all imposed. In its Draft document the Committee suggested that it might be appropriate to change this structure in the light of the following factors:

i   the need to reflect modern practice, i.e. the changing role of social workers, CPNs and other members of the multi-disciplinary team and the move to integrated management of health and social services staff;

ii   the nature of the Committee's overall proposals, in particular, the intention to recommend that the nearest relative's power to apply be removed, and the intention to recommend the involvement of a judicial body immediately after the period of assessment.

5.8. In the light of these factors the Committee suggested in its Draft that it might:

i   be necessary to consider whether the applicant should continue to be an approved social worker, or whether it might be appropriate to permit mental health workers from other professional backgrounds, but similarly trained in relation to the new mental health act, to be the applicant;

ii   be less important to demand independence;

iii   be sufficient to require the involvement of only two professionals.

5.9.   We received many comments on these questions from a wide variety of respondents and we now make the following recommendations.

The Number of Professionals

5.10.   Only a small number of respondents commented on the number of professionals but those who did were generally in favour of retaining three. We agree and therefore recommend that the involvement of three professionals should still be required. We take this view because:

i   although we are recommending a significant reduction in the period of compulsion authorised by the professionals, 7 days still constitutes a major infringement of an individual's rights;

ii   the administration of compulsory treatment will be permitted in certain circumstances during the 7 day period;

iii   the criteria for entry to compulsory assessment raise questions which would benefit from some discussion between professionals;

iv   the full involvement of the independent 'judicial' decision maker may not be engaged until 28 days have elapsed.

The Identity of the Applicant

5.11.   Strongly voiced arguments were expressed in favour of retaining the ASW as the applicant. These arguments include:

i   despite the increasing move towards integrated management, social workers retain an important element of independence, not least because they bring a non-medical perspective to bear, and independence remains an essential requirement;

ii   social workers perform an important co-ordinating role both before and after the assessment and typically deal with the social and domestic implications of an individual's admission to compulsion;

iii   social workers receive specific and rigorous training for the role.

5.12.   We appreciate, however, that for some respondents the arguments at 5.11.i. and 5.11.ii. were not very powerful. These respondents suggest that other mental health professionals are as capable of independence as ASWs, whatever their employment status, and until we know the results of current research we have no data on how, in practice, ASWs exercise their independence. These respondents also argue that the functions referred to in 5.11.ii. are not exclusive to ASWs.

5.13. There is a clear difference of opinion here which must be resolved. Thus on balance we recommend that, in the short term, the ASW is retained as the applicant but that consideration be given to the gradual extension of the role of applicant to include other mental health professionals who are not psychiatrists. This further consideration should take place in the knowledge of the relevant research findings. We would emphasise, however, that any additional professionals would have to be required to undergo specific training of equivalent rigour to that currently applying to ASWs.

The Other Two Professionals

5.14. We recommend that the other two professionals are:

i one medical practitioner, usually a psychiatrist from the trust providing specialist mental health services, with accredited training under the new act,

ii one other mental health professional who is either specifically trained or has knowledge of the patient.

5.15. Where applications for assessment under the new act are made to an independent hospital or nursing home, we recommend that restrictions similar to those set out in the 1983 Act are included, limiting those who can provide medical recommendations in support of such an application.

5.16. Elsewhere in this report we emphasise the crucial importance of adequate training for those specifically empowered under the new legislation, para 12.3-12.4. A continuing problem with the implementation of the 1983 Act has been the difficulty often encountered in trying to gain access to doctors approved under section 12. Whilst the cause of this problem is complex, its lack of resolution is unacceptable and it must not become a feature of the implementation of new legislation. We recommend that a clear duty be imposed on health authorities to ensure not only that an adequate number of approved doctors are available but also that arrangements are made to provide easy access when required.

5.17. In our Draft Proposals we suggested that the criteria for entry to compulsory assessment should mirror those currently imposed by section 2. However, we received several powerful submissions recommending the introduction of more stringent criteria. The view was expressed that if a broad diagnostic criterion, such as mental disorder, is adopted it becomes essential to ensure that the other criteria are sufficiently demanding to prevent the inappropriate use of compulsion, and possibly to guarantee compliance with the ECHR. We were also urged to recommend that the criteria for admission to assessment reflect those required for the eventual imposition of a compulsory order. We have found these arguments persuasive particularly in the light of the fact that we have decided to recommend that compulsory treatment for mental disorder be permitted during the assessment period in certain circumstances (see para 5.30-5.32)

5.18. We therefore recommend that the criteria be drafted in such a way as to include the following.

    i.   a person may be made subject to compulsory assessment if there are objective grounds to believe:

    ii.   that the patient is suffering from a mental disorder requiring care and treatment under the supervision of specialist mental health services;

and

    iii.   that, in the interests of the patient's health or safety or for the protection of others from serious harm or for the protection of the patient from serious exploitation, the mental disorder requires assessment;

and, either

    iv.   that the patient lacks the capacity to consent to care and treatment for mental disorder;

or

    v.   that the patient fulfills the criterion described at para 5.95.v.;

and

> vi.   that adequate assessment cannot be conducted in the absence of compulsory powers.

5.19.   It is important at this point to stress the need to ensure that these criteria are interpreted and applied in accordance with the principles of equality and respect for diversity at para 2.21. It is for this reason that we have recommended that there be 'objective' grounds for belief that the criteria are met. In addition it will be necessary to provide appropriate training to professionals, access to interpreters and access to independent advocacy. The obligation to monitor will also help to identify any anomalies.

The Formalities

5.20.   As is the case at present the three professionals would be required to complete statutory forms detailing their reasons for believing that the above criteria were fulfilled. There would be no absolute statutory obligation to consult the 'nominated person' (see paras 12.17-12.23) at this stage, although the advisability of doing so would be emphasised in the Code of Practice. The applicant would then lodge the forms with the appropriate authority within the trust/independent hospital, and the trust/independent hospital would become the formal compelling authority.

5.21.   In our Draft Proposals we suggested that that 'appropriate' authority should be an identified individual within senior management, known as the registered person, who would be empowered to appoint a deputy. In relation to the independent sector we recommend that the 'registered person' be the person or persons registered in respect of the hospital or mental nursing home under the Registered Homes Act 1984. We have received responses suggesting that the existing mental health act managers might continue to perform a role here but we have concluded that little is to be gained by such an addition. We would prefer to adopt as simple a model as possible and to place the responsibility clearly on an identified individual.

5.22.   The registered person, as is the position at present, would be required to scrutinise the documents to ensure that correct procedures had been followed and, if not so satisfied, would be unable lawfully to continue the process of compulsion.

5.23. In its Draft Proposals the Committee sought views on the advisability of providing for compulsory assessment outside hospital. The Draft explained that in line with our overall proposals we would like to recommend that the compulsory assessment power be available outside hospital as well as within hospital. If the specified tasks can be conducted outside a hospital setting and the necessary skilled practitioners are available then we would not wish to impose the requirement of hospital detention. In practice, given the absence of compliance, it may in many cases be necessary to detain the person in hospital in order to effect the assessment. But the Committee anticipates that there may be a number of cases where physical detention in hospital is not necessary and where assessment can more appropriately be effected elsewhere, at home, for example, or at a day centre. These cases may include both people for whom the transfer to hospital would be particularly traumatic, elderly people or children, for example, and those who are well known to services and are being supported in the community but whose condition is deteriorating.

5.24. Overall the responses received were in favour of breaking the automatic link between assessment and hospital: 'compulsory' assessment should be available outside hospital in those, possibly few, cases where it would be the most appropriate option. However, we appreciate the practical difficulties involved in empowering mental health professionals to enforce assessment outside hospital.

5.25. Thus we recommend that a distinction be made between **compulsory** and **formal** assessment. **Compulsory** assessment would only be carried out in hospital. In cases where hospital detention was not necessary or advisable the patient who fulfilled all the criteria listed above, para 5.18, apart from criterion 5.18.vi., should be told s/he had a choice. S/he could either comply with assessment in the community or come into hospital on a **compulsory** assessment. Assessment in the community would constitute a **formal** assessment and papers would be lodged with the trust/independent hospital in the same way. If the patient ceased to comply the assessment could be completed in hospital. In order to ensure that the choice between the two was made either voluntarily by the patient or, in cases of incapacity, in the patient's best interests, it would be necessary to have access to independent advocacy or, where available, the patient's advance agreement.

5.26. In its Draft Proposals the Committee asked for views on whether it should be possible to move directly to an application for a compulsory order without first engaging compulsory assessment. Most respondents who expressed a view considered that such a route should be open provided the necessary safeguards were in place. The Committee would suggest that the proposed **formal** assessment process should be used to provide the necessary safeguards in such cases.

The Period of Assessment

5.27. In its Draft Proposals the Committee suggested that the period of compulsory assessment should extend for a maximum of 7 days during which time a number of tasks would have to be conducted. At the end of that period, if the team wished to seek a compulsory order, an application would have to be made to an independent tribunal. The Committee also proposed that no compulsory treatment for mental disorder should be given during that period except in cases of emergency.

5.28. Many of the responses we received argued strongly that a 7 day period was too short a time to enable all the necessary work to be done in order to prepare for a full tribunal hearing. Some respondents also suggested that the prohibition on compulsory treatment, save in emergencies, was unwise and could have adverse effects for both patients and staff.

5.29. While we accept the force of these arguments, especially in relation to treatment, we are keen to encourage the active and prompt assessment of any individual on whom compulsion is imposed. We are also anxious to retain the concept of early intervention by an independent decision maker. We are therefore reaffirming our recommendation that an assessment order last for a maximum of 7 days, whether the assessment is compulsory or formal, during which time the tasks listed at para 5.32 are embarked upon. At any time during that period 'the clinical supervisor' (below para 5.34) must discharge the patient from compulsion if s/he no longer has grounds to believe the criteria are met. But if the team wish to extend compulsion beyond the 7 days the clinical supervisor must apply for confirmation of a provisional order to an independent body (see below), a significantly less demanding exercise than that envisaged in the initial proposals.

5.30. During the 7 day assessment emergency treatment powers would be available, see below paras 6.26 - 6.30, but the team would also be permitted to begin compulsory treatment for mental disorder (primarily medication) if, **either**

i. medication as part of a care and treatment plan of established efficacy had been approved by an independent decision maker within the last 6 months;

or

ii. the treatment was in accordance with an advance agreement, see below .

5.31. Treatment under 5.30.i. above should not, however, be available outside hospital in the case of a person subject to **formal** assessment. Any treatment given under the above provisions should be notified to the independent reviewer.

5.32. In the Draft Proposals the Committee listed a number of tasks which would have to be carried out by the multi-disciplinary care team, with the formal responsibility resting on the clinical supervisor. These tasks were generally approved by respondents and we list them now with some minor adjustments:

i. the assessment of the person's mental condition;

ii. the assessment of the person's physical condition, although consent would be necessary in cases where the person retained the relevant capacity;

iii. the assessment of risk in terms of both the seriousness of the feared harm and the likelihood (in terms of probability and imminence) of its occurrence or reoccurrence;

iv. the assessment of the person's capacity to consent to care and treatment for mental disorder;

v. the production of a proposed care and treatment plan;

vi. if feasible we would also wish to see a requirement imposed that, if the person does not object, there should be at least a preliminary assessment of his or her community care needs under section 47 NHS and Community Care Act 1990. This would help to inform the subsequent decision on the part of the independent decision maker, particularly with regard to the least restrictive alternative criterion (see below para 5.47);

vii. the assessment of the person's social and family circumstances.

5.33. During the period of assessment the care team would be required to notify and consult, where practicable, the nominated person, any involved carer (see below Chapter 11) and local advocacy services. For these purposes it would be necessary to identify the individual formally responsible within the team.

The Clinical Supervisor

5.34. In the Draft Proposals no express definition was provided of the term 'clinical supervisor' and the Committee is conscious of the need to remedy that omission. We are keen throughout to emphasise the relevance and value of non-medical perspectives in the field of mental health care and it is our intention to provide a structure which is designed to encourage multi-disciplinary working. Nonetheless, it is our understanding that the medical consultant is likely still to be regarded as retaining overall responsibility for the oversight of clinical care in which case s/he must retain the role of clinical supervisor. However, practice in this area is developing fast and there may well be occasions where the medical consultant would not be the most appropriate clinical supervisor, in the case of personality disorder for example. We therefore recommend that further thought be given to identifying a definition which is sufficiently flexible to reflect evolving practice.

Emergency Powers

5.35. Under the proposals outlined above admission to formal assessment would require the participation of three professionals. The Committee has received much evidence concerning the difficulties often faced in practice by those seeking to implement an urgent Mental Health Act assessment. The attendance of both ASWs and section 12 doctors can be very hard to achieve. While the Committee hopes that the situation will improve under the national service frameworks and certainly intends a full assessment by three professionals to be the normal process, it is convinced of the continuing need to provide for emergency powers of containment at least.

5.36. The 1983 Act provides for 72 hours emergency admission on the application of an ASW with one medical recommendation (section 4), for the imposition of detention on an in-patient for 72 hours on the basis of one medical recommendation (section 5(2)), and for a nurses' holding power of 6 hours (section 5(4)).

5.37. In our Draft Proposals we said that in the interests of simplicity we would like to see one emergency containment power which could be initiated, in relation to an in-patient in a mental health unit, by any duly trained and authorised social worker, nurse or medical practitioner as listed in the statute. While most respondents approved of the proposed simplification some concern was expressed about the need to ensure the ready availability of adequately trained nurses. It is our view that a registered mental health nurse or learning disability nurse with suitable additional training would be adequately trained to operate a 24 hour containment power and that one such a person should always be available within a hospital mental health unit. If the emergency arose in any place other than an in-patient mental health setting the involvement of both a mental health professional who is specially trained and a medical practitioner would be required.

5.38. In both cases, those involving psychiatric in-patients and in other situations, the emergency containment power would be available only in cases of urgent necessity and would authorise containment in hospital for a maximum of 24 hours. The fact of emergency containment and the reasons for it would be reported by the detainer to the registered person and to the MHAC or its successor body. During the period of containment only emergency treatment for mental disorder under the equivalent of section 62 (see below, para 6.26-27) would be permitted. If a compulsory assessment was not imposed by the end of that period the authority to detain would automatically lapse. If compulsory assessment was imposed the 7 days would start from the initial admission to emergency detention.

5.39. In addition the Committee recommends that the powers set out in section 136 and 135 of the 1983 Act be retained with the language modernised. The Committee has been urged to extend the section 136 powers of the police beyond a 'public place' but the Committee remains reluctant to do so. It would, however, like to see express confirmation that an Accident and Emergency Department is a public place for these purposes.

5.40. However, we now have a better understanding of the practical problems faced by the police. A police officer already possesses a power of forceable entry to private premises, under section 17 of the Police and Criminal Evidence Act 1984, for the purpose of saving life or limb. The problem the police face is their inability, after effecting entry under the 1984 Act, then to convey to a place of safety any person found in those premises who would otherwise fulfil the criteria of section 136. We therefore recommend that the successor to section 136 be drafted to provide the power to convey to a place of safety when a police officer has legitimately entered premises under section 17 Police and Criminal Evidence Act and has found a person there who would otherwise fall under section 136. We would not regard this extension as unjustifiably discriminatory since the power to enter is contained in a generally applicable statute and is not limited to mental disorder. We would, however, recommend that the police be required to record any such applications of the section and to send records annually to the MHAC successor body.

5.41. The Committee has heard strong arguments for removing the police station as a place of safety. However, in certain remote areas there may be no realistic alternative. We recommend instead that local protocols should continue to be developed so that normally the use of a police station is restricted to cases where there is a serious risk of violence. Further we recommend that an obligation be placed on Health Authorities to ensure the provision of and to certify specific places of safety other than police stations for section 136 purposes in their area.

5.42. The Committee can see no justification for allowing a longer period of detention under section 136 than under other emergency powers. It has to assume that current initiatives will be sufficient to deliver improved services. We therefore recommend that the successor to section 136 permit detention for up to 24 hours.

The Imposition of Longer Term Compulsion

5.43. The early introduction of independent decision making is central to the Committee's recommendations in this area. We are convinced that such a step will bring significant benefits in terms of the protection of patients' rights and thus compliance with the requirements of the ECHR, the consistent application of compulsion, improvements to the therapeutic relationship between patient and care team and the acceptability and thus effectiveness of the whole compulsory structure. We were therefore greatly reassured to learn from the responses received to our Draft Proposals that the notion of independent decision making had received overwhelming support from those who addressed it.

5.44. We nonetheless appreciate that by recommending the early introduction of an independent decision maker we are reversing a familiar policy and must therefore explain our reasoning.

The Case for Independent Decision Making

5.45. The need to provide for independent adjudication in relation to compulsory hospitalisation was recognised by the Mental Health Act 1959 which provided for the introduction of the mental health review tribunal (MHRT). In the forty years since then access to an independent body empowered to authorise discharge has come to be regarded as essential, if for no other reason than it is required by the ECHR and now the Human Rights Act.

5.46. In relation to admission to compulsion, however, the Percy Commission (*Report of the Royal Commission on the Law Relating to Mental Illness and Mental Deficiency 1954-75* (H.M.S.O. 1957) favoured reliance on the professional judgment of doctors and social workers in preference to what was seen as the rather formalistic approval by the magistrates. This preference for professional judgment was reflected in the Mental Health Acts of both 1959 and 1983. The structure which the Committee is now considering would depart from this familiar policy when dealing with the longterm admission of patients to compulsion and thus requires some clear justification.

5.47. The Committee considers that the introduction of an independent decision maker to confirm admission to compulsion is in principle desirable for the following reasons:

    i.   admission to compulsion involves a significant deprivation of an individual's rights, typically loss of liberty and, through the compulsory administration of treatment, loss of physical integrity. In a society which now places a high value on the protection of human rights it would appear to be essential that such decisions are taken openly and accountably by an independent body;

    ii.   the early intervention of an independent body would place the formal responsibility for compulsion outside the clinical team;

    iii.   it would provide a forum for the full participation of the patient at a crucial early stage in decision making about his or her treatment and care;

    iv.   the introduction of independent consideration would be reassuring to the patient, to the family and to carers;

    v.   it would improve the consistency of decision making;

    vi.   it would give to the tribunal the task of ensuring the protection of public safety by the imposition of the least restrictive alternative.

5.48. In the context of the specific scheme which the Committee is recommending the introduction of an independent decision maker is particularly important for the following reasons:

i   the Committee is aware of the very real concerns held by users, carers and mental health practitioners about the extension of compulsion to the community and it believes that the introduction of approval by an independent decision making process is essential if these fears are to be allayed;

ii   judicial imposition in one form or another is a common feature of the community treatment models in other jurisdictions;

iii   the introduction of judicial imposition would remove enduring concern over compliance with our obligations under the ECHR;

iv   the principles of non-discrimination and patient autonomy which the Committee regard as central promote the significance of capacity and best interests. Both these concepts are open to wide interpretation and the Committee considers it essential that their practical application be subject to independent review;

v   as conceived, the introduction of early independent decision making would require the clinical team not only to consider diagnosis and the need for compulsion, but to produce at an early stage detailed proposals as to care and treatment against which the patient's progress could be assessed.

5.49. The Committee recognises that the introduction of an independent body to confirm the imposition of compulsion would have significant resource implications, even under its revised proposals. However, it considers that there are considerable practical and structural advantages:

i   section 2 hearings under the current structure would be replaced by independent review at 7 days and the right to apply for an expedited hearing;

ii   the Committee is recommending the abolition of the managers' power to discharge;

iii   the Committee favours the creation of one independent body empowered to confirm the imposition, variation and renewal of an order, and to order discharge;

iv   the Committee also favours the transfer of the role currently performed by second opinion appointed doctors to the independent body (or at least to its medical member);

v   it is hoped that the introduction of the compulsory assessment process as described above followed by a provisional order will reduce the need to resort to longterm compulsion by making the assessment process more rigorous and by drawing patients into the discussion of their care and treatment at an early stage;

vi   in any event by delaying the automatic full tribunal hearing to day 28 we would anticipate a significant reduction in numbers: figures on the operation of the current Act for 1997/8 indicate that approximately 50% of all those people who enter compulsion under the civil provisions become informal before the 28 day point. We cannot estimate the proportion of patients who will seek an expedited tribunal, but approximately 20% of patients currently admitted under section 2 at present apply for a tribunal.

The Overall Structure

5.50.   In what follows we have tried to devise a structure which:

i   encourages good practice and the promotion of consensual care;

ii   thereby promotes public, patient and staff safety;

iii   provides sufficient independent oversight to protect the rights and interests of the patient, both those who are able and prepared to challenge and those who are not;

iv   does not impose unreasonable demands on professional time and resources.

5.51.   In all cases of compulsory or formal assessment authority to compel will cease unless the care team applies for a further order. In our Draft Proposals we recommended that at the end of the 7 days the care team would have to apply to a full tribunal which would have the power to approve a care and treatment order lasting up to six months. Many respondents argued that this time scale was unrealistic. Care teams would find it difficult to complete all the necessary assessments and patients would often be unable to organise proper representation within 7 days. We find these arguments persuasive and are not therefore intending to recommend such an early introduction of a full tribunal hearing. However, we remain convinced of the need for the introduction of some form of early, automatic independent review with the power to release the patient from compulsion.

5.52. We are of this view for the following reasons:

    i   we are anxious to encourage prompt and rigorous assessment by the care team once compulsion has been imposed and we believe independent review would be an important incentive;

    ii   we regard independent review as an essential safeguard against the inappropriate imposition of compulsion, however rare, and consider that it should be available automatically, its introduction should not be dependent on an initiative taken by the patient, as is currently the case with appeals under section 2.

5.53. However, we are of course aware of the implications of any review in terms of both professional time and resources. What we are now recommending would be essentially a paper exercise. A care team which wished to continue compulsion and start regular treatment would be required to apply for a provisional order. The criteria for such an order would mirror those described below in relation to the more longterm compulsory order. The application would be made on the basis of the completion of statutory forms which would require the necessary evidence to be specified. There would be no obligation to provide additional reports. The forms would be lodged with the registered individual who would be obliged to forward them immediately (electronically) to the independent reviewer. The lodging of the necessary documents with the registered individual would provide formal authority for continued compulsion, the role of the independent reviewer would be to confirm the order.

5.54. The independent review would be conducted by one individual (see below) who would be obliged to discharge the patient from compulsion if s/he was not satisfied that the evidence necessary to fulfil the criteria had been provided. In cases of uncertainty the reviewer could request further information from the team or could call on more expert colleagues for their advice (see below). In cases where the reviewer believed there to be serious doubts s/he could refer the case to an expedited tribunal.

5.55. Independent review would therefore apply in all cases where the compulsion lasted for over 7 days. In cases where the reviewer confirmed the provisional order and the patient mounted no challenge the provisional order would last for 21 days unless the patient was discharged by the clinical supervisor. If the care team wished to extend the compulsion after the 28th day (calculated from the beginning of formal or compulsory assessment) the clinical supervisor would have to apply for confirmation of a compulsory order by the full tribunal. On this occasion there would be an oral hearing and the patient would be entitled to legal representation. At such a hearing the tribunal's powers would include discharging the patient from compulsion by refusing to confirm the order and confirming a compulsory order of up to six months duration.

5.56. Thus the patient who took no active steps would receive an independent review at day 7 and a full tribunal hearing on day 28. We are, however, confident judging from experience of the existing system, that approximately 50% of patients entering compulsion will have become informal before day 28 in the natural course of events.

5.57. Where a patient wished actively to challenge the fact of compulsion we recommend that during the first 14 days s/he be entitled to request an expedited tribunal. The tribunal would then be under a duty to hear the patient's application within 7 days. Thus both a patient who wished to challenge from the outset and a patient whose further compulsion had been confirmed at independent review would have the opportunity to request an expedited hearing. At such a hearing the tribunal would possess all the powers available to it at the 28 day point.

5.58. We intend through this proposed structure to provide better safeguards than those which exist currently under the 1983 Act for all patients, whether or not they take active steps to challenge the compulsion, but to do so in such a way as to fulfil all the objectives listed at para 5.50.

The Constitution of the Independent Decision Makers

5.59. In the structure described above it is proposed to give significant roles to both an independent reviewer and a new tribunal. In our original Draft Proposals we described our early thinking on the constitution and membership of the tribunal. We will accordingly begin with our recommendations in relation to the tribunal itself.

The Tribunal

5.60. Under our revised proposals the tribunal would continue to perform a crucial role, although in the majority of cases it would only become involved from day 28. It is therefore essential that the tribunal be of an appropriate status, be properly skilled, trained, serviced and resourced. The Committee is convinced that this requires more than the mere extension of the existing MHRT.

5.61. In order to meet the requirements of article 5(4) the new tribunal must be independent of the detaining authority. We would therefore recommend that, as is the present case with the MHRT, appointments be made by the Lord Chancellor. We would further recommend that in order to emphasise its independence of both the Department of Health and the Home Office, and its status as a 'judicial' body, the tribunal be transferred to the Lord Chancellor's Department, subject to any necessary improvements in the administrative arrangements and to an adequate transfer of resources. Proper resourcing is essential if the body is to carry out its judicial functions satisfactorily. Tribunals, for example, must be adequately clerked.

5.62. In its Draft Proposals the Committee suggested that the new tribunal should be a national body, with a regional organisational structure and a national president. This recommendation met with considerable approval and the Committee now endorses it. We believe that a national presidential structure is essential in order to achieve the necessary consistency of decision making and the regular monitoring we describe below. It is a structure favoured for tribunals generally by the Council on Tribunals.

5.63. The new tribunal will be required to grapple with expert evidence in relation to mental disorder, treatment, risk and capacity, and to reach decisions which will invariably have profound effects on individual rights and occasionally serious implications for public safety. In order both to have and to inspire sufficient confidence the membership must be specifically and carefully trained. The Committee has received advice to the effect that the best way to achieve such training might be to introduce a statutory responsibility to train on the tribunal itself and to encourage reference to guidance from the Judicial Studies Board. Resources must be specifically allocated for training.

Membership

5.64. The present membership of the MHRT includes lawyers, psychiatrists and people with such experience, knowledge or qualification as the Lord Chancellor considers suitable, the so called lay members. In our Draft Proposals we suggested retaining both a medical and a legal membership. Nothing we have received by way of response has caused us to alter our views on the need to retain access to medical and legal expertise. We remain convinced that the tribunal must have ready access to its own source of medical expertise in order to achieve both the necessary quality of decision making and the confidence of the psychiatric profession. In some respects the question of the lawyer's role requires more careful justification. As a Committee containing a significant proportion of members from a legal background we have felt particularly vulnerable to the charge of encouraging a return to legalism. However, we can see no alternative to retaining a legal member. The tribunal must have a clear understanding of the statutory framework and the requirements of procedural fairness, it must be skilled in assessing the relative merits of the evidence and opinion presented and must be and appear to be entirely independent of the care team and detaining trust. While it might be suggested that any member given sufficient training could acquire the necessary skills, whatever their background, we suspect that the professional and institutional independence of a lawyer would be hard to replicate. In addition it is essential that the public have confidence in the system and to that end we would recommend, as is currently the case, that any tribunal considering the equivalent of a restricted case be chaired by a lawyer specially approved by the Lord Chancellor.

5.65. If the model of a three person panel is to be retained in any form, see below, we are anxious to ensure that the third member bring additional experience or expertise to the panel and has sufficient confidence to operate as an equal contributor. In our Draft Proposals we suggested that the third member should have knowledge of social service and community care provision. We consider that this is particularly important in the light of the possible application of the compulsory order outside hospital. However, we are equally conscious of the need to reflect the nature of the local population as far as possible in the membership of the tribunal, and we have also received powerful submissions concerning the need to include those with experience of the system either as users or carers. We would therefore recommend that the third member be someone with experience of mental health services outside hospital either as a professional, a carer or a user of those services, and we would emphasise again the importance of training. We do, however, appreciate the genuine concern over public safety in some cases and would recommend that thought be given to introducing a similar caveat here in the case of restricted patients as applies to the legal member. Thus in restricted cases the third member might be expected to have special expertise in the area of risk assessment.

Decision Making Model

5.66. While the nature of the skills and experience which must be available to the tribunal is relatively clear the precise nature of the preferred model of decision making is less straight forward. The model currently adopted by the MHRT is to constitute a three person multi-disciplinary panel, for each hearing, chaired by the legal member with the medical member conducting a prior assessment of the patient. The panel thus has the benefit of its own expert's direct opinion of the patient. While we can see certain advantages to this model in terms of convenience, we retain serious reservations in relation to the difficult dual role played by the medical member as both expert witness and decision maker. Similar reservations were expressed by the Council on Tribunals as long ago as 1983 (*Annual Report of the Council on Tribunals 1982-3 HMSO 1983).* Indeed it is our view that the role of the medical member cannot be maintained in its present form.

5.67. We have considered the possibility of retaining the medical member's duty separately to assess the patient and at the same time introducing a duty to report his/her conclusions openly to the tribunal. While we appreciate that this would go some way to meeting our concerns, we consider that the requirements of fairness can only fully be met if the patient or his/her representative is permitted to challenge the medical member through questioning. However, we suspect this option would prove unacceptable to medical members, with inevitable consequences for recruitment, and could potentially undermine the doctor's position as a full panel member. We therefore reject this as an option.

5.68. In our Draft Proposals we suggested, as one possible alternative, retaining the three person panel but removing from the medical member the obligation to assess the patient. Instead the tribunal would seek a report from an independent doctor selected from an approved panel. Such a doctor would examine the patient and provide both a written and oral report to the tribunal. However, as we recognised, such a model would be very costly, particularly with regard to consultant time. It would typically demand the participation of two consultant psychiatrists in addition to the patient's own clinical supervisor. In the light of the many contributions we have received pointing to the severe shortage of psychiatrists we fear that such a model, whatever its intrinsic merits, would not be workable, even with the postponement of hearings in most cases to day 28 rather than day 7 as in our initial proposals.

5.69. It would be possible to adapt this model by replacing the automatic independent medical opinion with a power in the tribunal to seek one where necessary. However, we fear this would increase the likelihood of delays and adjournments.

5.70. A further alternative which would meet both the demands of fairness and the problem of the lack of doctors would be to constitute a tribunal without a medical member. The tribunal would then have access to a panel of approved independent doctors, and could select a doctor from within the relevant specialism to examine the patient and the proposed care and treatment and report to the tribunal. The selected doctor could also assist the tribunal in examining the medical records, and in questioning the care team and any expert commissioned by the patient. S/he would not however be a member of the decision making team and would not retire with them. In addition independent doctors from the approved panel would be available to perform the functions in relation to the approval of specific treatments described below in Chapter 6.

5.71. This model could operate either with a three person tribunal consisting of a legal chair and two trained non-psychiatrist members with the expertise etc described above, or with a single person 'tribunal'. We would envisage that such a single person model would involve a specially trained lawyer who would have access as suggested to a panel of medical experts. S/he could also have access to a parallel panel of independent experts in the provision of community services and/or risk assessment. While the three person model has the advantage of involving a breadth of expertise directly in the decision making, it may be less acceptable to the psychiatric profession if psychiatry alone among the relevant disciplines is to be excluded from full membership. The single person model avoids this difficulty but may be regarded as unorthodox in terms of normal tribunal practice and may place too heavy a burden on one individual.

5.72. As a way of achieving the necessary independence and expertise while at the same time reflecting both the demands of fairness and the realities of consultant availability we favour the model of the tribunal without a medical member, but with access to independent medical advice. If this is accepted we would consider that the final choice between the three person and the one person panel can only be made on the basis of further consultation with the relevant interests, including the Royal College of Psychiatrists and the Council on Tribunals.

5.73. Following *Who Decides?* and *Bournewood*, it is most likely that an independent body will eventually be required to approve certain decisions in relation to longterm incapacitated adults. In considering the precise form of such a body we strongly recommend that early thought be given to the creation of a single 'tribunal' with sufficient expertise and flexibility to operate in relation to both mental disorder and longterm incapacity. There would be great advantage in concentrating expertise and administration in one body and, therefore, we recommend that if any new tribunal is established, this wider context be born in mind.

5.74. Whatever the precise form finally taken by the tribunal, an oral hearing will be required at the 28 day point, at any expedited hearing, at any application by the care team for renewal or variation or by the patient for discharge. Further, legal representation and legal aid in the current form will have to be available for all oral hearings and will have to cover the provision of an independent second medical opinion at the request of the patient. Such second opinions could be drawn from the approved panel described above. We also recommend that, in consultation with the Law Society and the Legal Aid Board, further thought be given to the need to ensure the availability of sufficient solicitors, particularly in rural areas.

5.75. We are aware of the difficulties currently encountered by both clinical staff and tribunal members by the frequent demands of tribunals, and recommend that consideration be given to establishing a regular day of the week on which tribunals would be held in particularly busy hospitals. If this did prove valuable then the time limits etc would have to be carefully drafted to take account of the possibility.

5.76. We recommend that the tribunal be required to adopt inquisitorial procedures, the details of which should be provided by way of statutory instrument as at present.

5.77. A right of appeal on point of law should, in our view, be provided to the High Court and judicial review would continue to be available. We also recommend that the tribunal be empowered to refer a case directly to the High Court, Family Division for a decision on the merits. This power would form an important link between the two jurisdictions and might be used to clarify questions arising as to whether a particular treatment was for a mental or a physical disorder, for example, or as to the capacity or best interests of a child.

5.78. The power should only be available in exceptional circumstances but, if exercised sparingly would have the beneficial effects of:

i   accelerating access to the High Court

ii   avoiding duplication of proceedings

iii   enhancing the status of the tribunal system.

5.79. It should also ensure that the quality of decision making in the tribunal is subject to consideration and comment by the High Court other than in the restricted context of an appeal on a question of law, or when considering an application for judicial review.

5.80. We have emphasised the importance we attach to the adequate training of tribunal members and we recommend that a system of regular accreditation be introduced. It is also essential to ensure an acceptable system of monitoring. The tribunal will be subject to the supervisory jurisdiction of the High Court in individual cases and the Council on Tribunals will maintain its role in terms of general oversight. In addition we would like to recommend the introduction of a more comprehensive form of performance monitoring. We appreciate that there are sensitivities here with regard to judicial independence and compliance with the ECHR. However we consider that with the introduction of a national presidential structure there is scope for the introduction of a duty to monitor on the tribunal itself. Such a framework would be in line with the recommendations of the *Council on Tribunals* (1997, Cm 3744)

The Independent Reviewer

5.81. The proposed structure of compulsion introduces independent review by day 7. We see this review both as an incentive to prompt and rigorous assessment and as an essential safeguard to patients. We do not, however, wish to introduce an automatic oral hearing at this early stage and would envisage the review as essentially a paper or electronic exercise. It follows that the reviewer must have sufficient status and professional confidence to reject the care team's request for a 21 day order if sufficient grounds are not made out in the documents.

5.82. Our preference would be to see the reviewing task performed by a legal member of the tribunal. Since it could be done at a distance, the particular member could be one of a number, possibly the duty member 'on call' at the regional office, and there should be no difficulty in ensuring that the reviewer had no further contact with the case were that thought to be important. We appreciate that this preliminary reviewing role might not conform to orthodox tribunal practice but we see it as akin to certain interlocutory functions performed by other judicial bodies and can see no reason in principle why it should conflict with the tribunal's primary role.

5.83. Our priority is to introduce an early safeguard for patients which is of sufficient independence and status to inspire confidence and at the same time as undemanding as possible in terms of extra resources.

5.84. As suggested above the reviewer should have the power to request further information from the care team, to consult expert colleagues and, in exceptional circumstances, to call for an expedited tribunal, giving adequate time for all to prepare. If the reviewer were a tribunal member the power to consult could be exercised by simply referring to experts on the approved panels.

The Compulsory Orders

5.85. The proposed structure envisages a two stage process:

i   at 7 days, or earlier with the patient's consent, the provisional order lasting 21 days;

ii   at 28 days, or earlier if an expedited hearing is requested, the compulsory order lasting a maximum of 6 months.

5.86. Both orders must be sought by the clinical supervisor and the outcome must be reported to the successor body to the MHAC.

The Provisional Order

5.87. If the care team wishes to extend compulsion beyond 7 days the clinical supervisor must apply for a provisional order. Such an order would permit the start of a care and treatment programme whether in hospital or in the community.

5.88. In order to establish the case for such an order the clinical team through the completion of appropriate statutory forms would have to supply evidence that the tasks required during the assessment period were either completed or well underway and that there was evidence to support the fulfilment of the statutory criteria. In cases where treatment had already begun the reasons for that would also have to be provided. These forms would be lodged simultaneously with the registered person and the independent reviewer.

5.89. If the independent reviewer was satisfied 'on the evidence currently available' that the statutory criteria described below were met, s/he would so indicate to the registered person and authority to compel would be confirmed. If the independent reviewer was conclusively not so satisfied, s/he would so inform the registered person and the patient would be discharged from all compulsion. In any of the cases of doubt described above at para 5.54, the lodging of the papers with the registered person would provide the necessary authority to detain and treat, on the basis available during a compulsory assessment, pending a final outcome.

The Compulsory Order

5.90. In all cases where a provisional order had been granted and the care team wished to extend the period of compulsion beyond the 28th day and in all cases where an expedited hearing was requested the care team would have to apply for a compulsory order. The application would be lodged with the registered person who would be obliged to forward it (electronically) to the tribunal.

5.91. Once in receipt of an application the tribunal would have the following options:

    i   to confirm a compulsory order which would specify place of containment/residence and require compliance on the part of the patient with the approved care and treatment plan. In the first instance the order would last for a maximum of 6 months and could be renewed on application by the clinical team for one further 6 month period, and subsequently for a maximum of twelve months;

    ii   to refuse to confirm the order, in which case the patient would be discharged from all compulsion;

5.92. In our Draft Proposals we envisaged the possibility that patients with longterm incapacity by reason of a learning disability or similar condition should be diverted at this point to the alternative framework under *Who Decides?* We still regard this as the appropriate outcome and would hope that by the time any new mental health legislation is introduced there is a comprehensive framework for those with longterm incapacity. If this is not the case then it may, unfortunately, be necessary to use the new mental health structure, however inadequate that would be. We are not at this stage inclined to recommend the introduction of interim guardianship provisions.

5.93. The compulsory order would be applicable to patients within or outside hospital.

5.94. In what follows we have not attempted to achieve the precision of statutory drafting. Rather we have tried to convey the meaning we would like to see reflected within the statutory language. We would, however, like to emphasise the need to make the language accessible to those non-lawyers who will be responsible for its daily interpretation.

5.95. Before confirming a compulsory order the tribunal would have to be satisfied as to the following:

  i.   the presence of mental disorder which is of such seriousness that the patient requires care and treatment under the supervision of specialist mental health services;

  and

  ii.   that the care and treatment proposed for, and consequent upon, the mental disorder is the least restrictive and invasive alternative available consistent with safe and effective care;

  and

  iii. that the proposed care and treatment is in the patient's best interests;

  and, either

  iv.   that, in the case of a patient who lacks capacity to consent to care and treatment for mental disorder, it is necessary for the health or safety of the patient or for the protection of others from serious harm or for the protection of the patient from serious exploitation that s/he be subject to such care and treatment, and that such care and treatment cannot be implemented unless s/he is compelled under this section;

  or

  v.   that, in the case of a patient who has capacity to consent to the proposed care and treatment for her/his mental disorder, there is a substantial risk of serious harm to **the health or safety of the patient or to** the safety of other persons if s/he remains untreated, and there are positive clinical measures included within the proposed care and treatment which are likely to prevent deterioration or to secure an improvement in the patient's mental condition.

5.96. The distinction made between patients who have the capacity to make treatment decisions and those who do not, reflected in criteria 5.95.iv. and 5.95.v., is central to our desire to produce a non-discriminatory and principled framework for intervention in the absence of consent. As we explain in Chapter 2, we wish to enable care and treatment to be given in the interests of the patient's health and safety where the patient lacks the capacity to consent, but where the patient retains that capacity and is objecting we consider that the justification for compulsory intervention does not extend that far. In paras 2.8-2.10 we describe two possible approaches to this dilemma in relation to harm to self.

5.97. The words emboldened in criterion 5.95.v. would be omitted if a consistent approach to autonomy were to be adopted. According to such an approach the only justification for overriding the principles of non-discrimination and patient autonomy would be the need to protect others from a substantial risk of serious harm. In cases where a patient maintained a capable refusal of care and treatment compulsory intervention would not be justified solely to protect the patient. On the other hand, the emboldened words would remain if a more pragmatic approach were to be adopted. Such an approach would allow intervention for the protection of the patient in cases of severe risk.

5.98. Whichever approach is adopted, consistent or pragmatic, however, we are persuaded that a health statute can only authorise the overriding of patient autonomy if there is a health intervention of likely efficacy available. We therefore strongly recommend the inclusion of the concept contained in the final phrase of criterion 5.95.v. To do otherwise would be to require health service professionals to engage in activities which they would regard as inappropriate and possibly unethical.

5.99. In our original proposals we suggested in the equivalent to 5.95.v. the phrase 'medical treatment for mental disorder from which the patient is likely to benefit', but we now consider that such words could still lead to the uncertainties of definition connected with the current treatability test. On the one hand they could be used by doctors to exclude those they found hard to treat with drugs, while on the other the words could still be interpreted very widely to include merely containment in a therapeutic environment.

5.100. It is our firm expectation that the majority of patients falling to be considered under criterion 5.95.v. will be those suffering from a personality disorder either alone or in combination with other forms of mental disorder. We base this expectation on the belief that most 'mentally ill' patients who present the required level of risk will not retain the necessary capacity. We are therefore keen to develop a form of words which, while encompassing the notion of a positive clinical intervention, is not limited to pharmacological treatments. We want to encourage psychological interventions but also to avoid a form of words which can be interpreted so broadly as to permit merely therapeutic containment. We therefore suggest: 'there are positive clinical measures included within the proposed care and treatment which are likely to prevent deterioration or to secure improvement in the patient's mental condition.' We appreciate that the drafting is not ideal, but hope that it conveys our intentions.

5.101. These criteria at para 5.95, would apply equally to compulsion within and outside hospital. It would be up to the care team to specify within the proposed care and treatment the appropriate location and the reasons for it.

5.102. The notion of capacity which is central to the criteria will require careful definition and guidance. A possible definition is discussed in Chapter 7. The notion of best interests in criterion 5.95.iii. is discussed at Chapter 8.

5.103. In addition to the need to define key concepts, it would also be necessary to provide guidance indicating what evidence might be required in order to establish certain aspects of the criteria. It would, for example, be essential to indicate the nature of the risk assessment required in order to investigate the presence of sufficient risk to satisfy criterion 5.95.v. and it might be advisable to introduce a standard risk assessment format. We would recommend specific consultation on this issue.

5.104. With regard to community orders particularly it would be necessary to require evidence of a history of failure to accept the proposed care and treatment in order to establish criterion 5.95.iv.. The tribunal might also be directed towards investigating the degree of confidence possessed by the care team that the mere fact of the compulsory order will persuade the patient to co-operate. Cases where physical resistance is anticipated would not be appropriate for a community order and would not fulfil criterion 5.95.ii.

5.105. Where the compulsory order relates to treatment in hospital the need to safeguard the patient's remaining rights and freedoms is dealt with above, paras 3.29 – 3.32. Where the order relates to care and treatment outside hospital, the order itself will be required to specify the obligations on all parties.

5.106. A compulsory order relating to care and treatment outside hospital may contain detailed provisions in relation to the following:

    i   identification of the services which the health or social services NHS Trust or other service provider is required to provide under the principle of reciprocity;

    ii   place of residence and obligation to report any change of address. A number of reservations have been expressed to us concerning the inclusion of place of residence as a possible condition. It has been suggested that such a condition could discriminate against those who have no 'suitable' housing. It is our view that in practice those without adequate housing are unlikely to be considered for community treatment in any event until accommodation is found and if, in exceptional circumstances, they were to be so considered the condition could be omitted. It would not be mandatory. The problem does not lie in the inclusion of the condition but in the scarcity of supervised accommodation. Finally it should be emphasised that under the proposed structure any civil patient who ceased to fulfil the statutory criteria for compulsion would be entitled to be discharged from all compulsion, both hospital and community based.

    iii   the nature of the proposed care and treatment and the location where such care and treatment is to take place;

    iv   the obligation on the patient to allow access and to present him or her self for visits by identified case workers. The parallel obligation on the care team to keep to any such arrangements would broadly be covered by the obligations flowing from reciprocity;

    v   the consequences of non-compliance with the conditions on the part of the patient, which could include:

        • the power to convey to the place of care and treatment;

- the power of entry by an identified member of the care team;

- the power to convey to hospital.

5.107. In our Draft Proposals we suggested that a requirement to submit to drug testing through the provision of samples might be included. In the light of the responses received we are now of the view with regard to proscribed drugs that any such requirement must be with the consent of the patient and we would suggest that it would be better dealt with by way of an advance agreement with the patient. The patient would be aware that any return to drug use which led to a deterioration in his or her mental state could provide grounds for re/admission to hospital.

5.108. The question of compulsory medication in the community is extremely controversial and there are very real safety concerns relating to the forcible administration of medication outside a hospital setting. Under the scheme outlined in our Draft Proposals we suggested that in the face of persistent refusal to accept medication the clinical supervisor would have to decide whether to apply for an emergency variation of the order. Such a variation could permit the patient to be conveyed to or admitted to hospital, or in carefully defined circumstances could permit the administration of medication within an appropriate and safe non-hospital setting.

5.109. In the light of the responses we have received we now take the view that it would be preferable if the initial order included the power to convey or to admit the patient to hospital in the face of non-compliance with any of the conditions leading to a deterioration in the patient's mental health. The criteria for the two types of order are essentially the same. This ready flexibility would avoid the need specifically to empower the clinical supervisor to 'detain' the patient pending the outcome of any application to vary the order. Such detention if it were not in hospital might be perilous for the patient and the care team and would be vulnerable to legal challenge. We would recommend instead that the initial order permit re/admission to hospital in certain circumstances. In order to comply with the Human Rights Act the re/admitted patient would then have to have the right to challenge any such detention before the tribunal as a matter of urgency.

5.110. In any case where a re/admission to hospital had been required the care team could apply for a variation back into the community once the patient had recovered sufficiently. However, the tribunal would have to be satisfied that there was sufficient evidence to suggest that compliance with the order in the community was now likely, see above.

5.111. This proposal conceives of conveyance to hospital as the primary means of ensuring compliance with the order, particularly as regards co-operation with medication. In some cases of non co-operation with medication it might be sufficient to convey the patient to a hospital out-patient clinic, but in the face of persistent non co-operation leading to deterioration in the patient's mental state we would anticipate that in-patient admission would be required.

5.112. We understand, and to a large extent share, the desire to break the invariable link between compulsion and hospital detention, and for that reason we are content to recommend the introduction of authority to administer compulsory medication in a hospital out-patient setting providing all the criteria for compulsion are met. However, we are not satisfied that the necessary services are yet in place within the community to render the forcible administration of medication in a non-hospital setting either safe or advisable. We have not yet had the opportunity to consider the substance of the Mental Health National Service Framework and cannot therefore recommend such a significant extension of compulsory treatment powers at present. Instead we recommend that once the nature of the National Service Framework is known that the government engage in further consultation with the relevant interests to establish the practicality of any such extension in the context of the anticipated level of service provision within the community.

5.113. In our Draft Report we mentioned the submissions we had received to the effect that the anticipated difficulties of ensuring co-operation with medication in the community might encourage doctors to prescribe depot medication in place of the newer drugs, which have to be taken orally, even where the latter might be clinically preferred. Clearly any such distorting effect would have to be avoided. The principle of reciprocity demands that where an individual is being obliged to accept treatment that treatment be of an appropriate standard. However, in some cases it will be necessary to achieve a sensitive balance between the patient's best interests, the identification of the least restrictive and invasive alternative and the legitimate concerns of public safety. We consider that the tribunal will be best placed to attempt to achieve such a balance and we recommend that tribunals be required to take these issues into account when considering any proposed care and treatment plan in the community.

5.114. The consequences of non-compliance with the conditions of the order would have to be specified in the original order as described above. Ultimately in the face of persistent non-compliance the clinical team will have to decide whether to discharge the patient from the order, admit the patient to hospital or apply for a variation in order to reflect what is achievable.

5.115. It would be important to keep police involvement to an absolute minimum in order to reduce stigmatisation and confrontation and to make proper use of scarce police resources. Persistent resistance on the part of a patient should usually result either in the variation of the contentious condition or in admission to hospital, preferably in an ambulance accompanied by a mental health professional.

5.116. Where the care team do wish to enforce specific conditions, such as attendance at a place of treatment, the team, through the clinical supervisor, may in exceptional circumstances have to decide whether to enlist the assistance of the police. Local protocols would need to be in place to govern policy in such cases. Similarly if a patient went absent from the stipulated place of residence a decision would have to be made on the basis of a risk assessment whether to request police help in the patient's return. Sections 137 and 138 of the 1983 Act provide a possible model for the necessary powers.

The Ending of Compulsion

Compulsory Assessment

5.117. As stated above compulsory assessment would run for a maximum of 7 days. At the end of that period all compulsion will lapse automatically unless the clinical supervisor applies for a provisional order. It should not be permissable for the patient to be readmitted to compulsory assessment until a minimum period has elapsed. Within the compulsory assessment period the clinical supervisor may end the order at any time by reporting that fact and the reasons for it to the registered person. He or she would also be required to inform the successor body to the MHAC.

The Provisional Order

5.118. This order would last for a maximum of 21 days at the end of which period compulsion would lapse automatically unless the clinical supervisor had sought and the tribunal had confirmed a compulsory order. As with compulsory assessment the clinical supervisor could discharge the patient from compulsion at any time and the same reporting requirements would apply.

The Compulsory Order

5.119. A compulsory order will be specified to last for a fixed period. In the first instance the clinical supervisor may apply for and the tribunal may confirm a compulsory order of any duration up to a maximum of six months. On first renewal the 6 month maximum would still apply, but subsequently the order could last for up to 12 months. A renewal may only be confirmed by the tribunal on the application of the clinical supervisor.

5.120. We recommend that the clinical supervisor retain a power to grant leave of absence from hospital equivalent to that contained within section 17 of the current Act. The clinical supervisor should also retain the power to transfer a civil patient between hospital trusts. Any such transfers should be reported to the tribunal and the patient should have the right to apply to the tribunal on arrival at the new hospital if s/he considers there has been any substantial change in the way her/his care and treatment is delivered.

5.121. At any stage during the course of the order the clinical supervisor may discharge the patient from the order, and would indeed be obliged to do so if the patient no longer fulfilled the admission criteria. In our Draft Proposals we suggested that such a discharge might only be effected with the approval of the tribunal. We were anxious to deter the premature discharge of patients with inadequate provision for ongoing care. We remain keen to pursue this objective but appreciate that any suggestion that a patient's discharge might be delayed by the tribunal purely to ensure the provision of ongoing care could be vulnerable to legal challenge. We, therefore, recommend that the clinical supervisor be required to report any discharge to the tribunal together with details of the agreed ongoing care. This ongoing care would be offered informally, the patient would be under no obligation to accept, see paras 3.7 – 3.10. The tribunal would be asked to confirm the content and duration of the care package and where it was not satisfied it would have the power to request further information from the trust/independent hospital, in much the same way as the trial court is empowered to call for details of hospital provision under section 39 of the 1983 Act. In the vast majority of cases this process of clarification and confirmation would be conducted either on paper or electronically. We also recommend that a similar obligation to report ongoing care arrangements to the tribunal apply in cases where an order is allowed to lapse and no renewal is sought.

5.122. In view of the fact that we are recommending the recognition of a right in the patient to receive the services agreed in the ongoing care plan, we regard it as essential that the content of that plan be formally expressed and agreed.

5.123. At any time during the duration of the compulsory order the clinical supervisor would have the power to apply to the tribunal for a variation. He or she could, for example, apply to convert an order specifying treatment in hospital into an order which would apply outside hospital.

5.124. A patient who is the subject of a compulsory order of three months or more should have the right to apply to the tribunal for discharge on one occasion during the currency of the order. That right may be exercised by the nominated person on the patient's behalf. We have received submissions suggesting that the tribunal hearing such an application for discharge should not have the same membership as the tribunal which initially confirmed the order. While we see the force of this suggestion and consider that ideally the tribunals should be differently constituted, we are aware of the fact that MHRT members may currently sit on successive panels hearing applications from the same patient. We would therefore recommend that while a different panel should be constituted where possible, it should not be an absolute requirement because of the difficulties it might create in more remote areas.

5.125. In our Draft Proposals we suggested that in the light of the tribunal's early involvement through the confirmation of all compulsory orders it would no longer be necessary to provide for an automatic reference to the tribunal as at present. We now confirm that recommendation.

5.126. We also suggested that the tribunal should no longer retain the power to review cases on its own initiative. Our desire here was to protect the tribunal from frequent requests to exercise that power and we suggested instead that the successor body to the MHAC be given the power to refer cases to the tribunal. We have received responses suggesting both that the possession of 'own motion' powers by tribunals can be very useful and that the MHAC successor body might not welcome the additional pressure that the possession of a power to refer would place upon it. While we have no strong desire to remove the power of the tribunal to act on its own motion, we do consider that the MHAC successor body should have the power to refer cases, particularly in the light of our recommendation in relation to informal patients without the capacity to consent to care and treatment. We therefore recommend that further consultation on these issues be conducted with the relevant bodies.

5.127. In our Draft Proposals we indicated our intention to recommend the removal of the managers' power to discharge. In the main this proposal attracted considerable support. There has been some concern that the existence of two mechanisms for the review of detention has both been confusing to patients and has tended to impose considerable burdens on the clinical team with little obvious benefit to the patient in terms of early discharge. It was also suggested that under the proposed structure which would involve independent decision making automatically at a much earlier stage, there would be no justification for providing for a review by the managers as well.

5.128. There were, however, those who supported a continuing role for managers. It was argued that managers provide an important lay element and a link with the local community. It was also suggested that a managers' hearing provides a uniquely informal occasion at which the patient is able to hear the opinion of the care team. While we appreciate the strength of these arguments we would hope that the added emphasis we place on the role of independent advocacy at crucial stages in the process, together with the changes proposed to the role currently played by the nearest relative would inject an important independent lay element. We are also emphasising throughout the vital importance of negotiating agreement between the patient and the care team wherever possible and we are specifically recommending that an attempt be made to negotiate an advance agreement in every case when a patient comes to the end of a period of compulsion. It is hoped in this way to encourage more dialogue between the care team and the patient as matter of course, in which case it becomes less necessary to provide an additional forum by way of a mangers' hearing.

5.129. We, therefore, confirm our preliminary recommendation that the managers' power to discharge be removed. As we described above, para 5.20, the trust/independent hospital will be the detaining authority and at the start of the period of assessment will have the power, and in certain circumstances, the duty to discharge. This function will be exercised through the registered person on behalf of the trust/independent hospital. The trust/independent hospital through the registered person will also receive applications from the clinical supervisor for provisional and compulsory orders and for renewal of the latter. However, in view of the fact that an independent decision maker will be required to confirm those orders at the outset we do not consider it necessary, in terms of either good practice or our obligations under the Human Rights Act, to provide the registered person with the power to discharge at that stage.

5.130. In our Draft Proposals we recommended that it should be open to the tribunal, when asked to confirm a renewal or when hearing an application for discharge, to vary the order. Thus, rather than renewing an order which included detention in hospital, the tribunal would be free to direct a variation which would enable the necessary care and treatment to be provided outside hospital. At present the MHRT possesses no such power in relation to the supervised discharge.

5.131. In general this recommendation met with a favourable response but certain reservations were expressed concerning its practicality. These related mainly to the difficulties which might arise if a tribunal were to order the variation to a community order with which either the care team disagreed or on which social services had not been consulted. In answer it is important to emphasise that the tribunal would have to have a care and treatment programme before it which it could confirm as fulfilling the statutory criteria; the tribunal could not devise the programme itself. Thus in cases where the tribunal wished to consider a community order as an alternative to either a further hospital order or a discharge it would be empowered to adjourn and to ask the care team to devise an alternative programme. Clearly, if in either case the compulsion criteria were not met, the tribunal would have no alterative but to discharge in any event.

5.132. The Committee recommends that there be an obligation on the tribunal to report all decisions to the MHAC successor body.

5.133. Finally the Committee would like to recommend that the criteria for discharge are articulated in such a way as to reflect the criteria for admission to compulsion and that the tribunal be obliged to discharge unless satisfied that the criteria for admission continue to be met.

6. TREATMENT

6.1.   It is impossible to avoid the term treatment in any legislation concerned with its compulsory imposition. However, it does not follow that the term requires a specific statutory definition. Under the present Act the term is defined very broadly to include 'care, habilation and rehabilitation under medical supervision', section 145. This combined with the notion of treatability has given rise to an unfortunate lack of clarity.

6.2.   We explained in our Draft Proposals that, although we were keen to recognise the importance of a broad understanding of treatment which includes care and support and is not over dependent on the medical model, we did not wish to see a specific definition contained in any new legislation. Instead we favoured the imposition of special safeguards on certain types of treatment. In the main this proposal was favourably received by our respondents and we are inclined now to endorse it. However, it carries certain implications with which we now deal.

6.3.   At present Part IV of the 1983 Act distinguishes between treatments which can be administered in the absence of either consent or second opinion (section 63), those which require consent or second opinion (section 58), and those which require both consent and second opinion (section 57). In our Draft Proposals we suggested that we would not recommend any substantive change to the effect of section 63 and 57. While that remains true of section 57 we now take the view that section 63 in its present form should be abandoned.

6.4   Under our proposed scheme each patient placed under a compulsory order will be subject to approved care and treatment related specifically to his or her mental disorder. It is our intention that all the forms of 'medical treatment' currently covered by section 63 could be included either expressly or by implication within the approved care and treatment. While it would certainly not be necessary for the clinical team to itemise specifically all forms of care, the process of approval by the tribunal would help to ensure that all proposed interventions were directly related to the mental disorder from which the patient was suffering.

6.5.   This approach would help to relieve some of the problems raised by respondents in relation to section 63 and the patient who retains capacity. In such cases the approved care and treatment would be designed to reflect the patient's wishes in so far as the structure permitted those to prevail. This issue is considered further below. It would also permit recognition, on the same basis, of a patient's preferences expressed in any advance agreement.

6.6.   In recent years there have been problems with identifying the limits of treatment 'for mental disorder'. We would anticipate that under the new structure any such uncertainties which arose at the outset would be dealt with by the tribunal in confirming the proposed care and treatment. Uncertainties which arose during the course of an order should be referred by the clinical supervisor to the tribunal, or at least to the independent doctor, who would then be empowered to call for a full tribunal hearing. The tribunal in turn, if unable to resolve the issue, should be empowered to refer the case directly to the High Court, Family Division for a decision on the merits, above para 5.77-78.

6.7.   The other context in which the definition of treatment is currently controversial is in relation to the treatability test. We have described above our intentions in this regard which will not involve the need to define treatment.

6.8.   We move now to considering those treatments in relation to which we recommend the application of special safeguards.

Neurosurgery for Mental Disorder and Other Specially Invasive Treatments

6.9.   The Committee would like to recommend that essentially the same safeguards as those which currently apply under section 57 be maintained in relation to neurosurgery. At present under that section the Secretary of State has the power to add further specified treatments and he has done so in relation to 'the surgical implantation of hormones for the purposes of reducing male sex drive'. We recommend that both the power to add treatments and the above addition be retained.

Medication

6.10.   At present medication for mental disorder may be given to a detained patient in the absence of consent for a period of 3 months. After that period the treating doctor is required either to certify consent or to obtain a second opinion certification under section 58. The Committee is convinced of the need to provide a framework for the authorisation of medication in the absence of consent (both where there is no capacity to consent and occasionally where there is a capable refusal), however, the initial submissions received contained much criticism of the present structure.

6.11.   Under the overall structure which we are now recommending, the proposed care and treatment would require approval by the tribunal at the outset, or by the independent reviewer in the case of the provisional order. In our Draft Proposals we recommended that the existing three month rule be reduced to two months. Thus after two months of medication, dating from the first approval of the care and treatment, the clinical team would be required to apply for a 'second opinion' in order to authorise the continuation of the treatment. Some of those who responded to this proposal queried the selection of two rather than three months and others suggested that even within that period the clinical supervisor should be entitled to seek a 'second opinion'. In the time available to us we have been unable to consult adequately on the preferred time limit. We are aware of the strongly held view that three months is unnecessarily long but we have been unable to identify the most widely accepted alternative. We recommend that further consultation is required here to establish the best period on the basis of all available research. We also recommend that once that period is identified it is expressed in such a way as to entitle the clinical supervisor to invoke a 'second opinion' earlier if required.

6.12.   In our Draft Proposals we suggested that this 'second opinion' function might sensibly be performed by a medical member of the tribunal. To the extent that this proposal was designed to simplify matters and to avoid the necessity as at present of maintaining two distinct lists of doctors, it attracted widespread approval. It would obviate the need for the MHAC to appoint second opinion appointed doctors (SOADs). However, we appreciate the concerns which were expressed about the apparent lack of independence if the same doctor were both to act on the tribunal which approved the order and to provide the second opinion. We therefore recommend that the statute be worded in such a way as to ensure this could not happen. If the model of a tribunal with no medical member is accepted the same panel of approved doctors could be used both to advise the tribunal and to perform second opinions, provided no duplication of function in individual cases was allowed.

6.13.   If the tribunal doctor is to fulfil the function of the SOAD under section 58 the Committee considers that the tribunal should also provide the doctor for section 57 approval. The other two members of the team could be taken from the MHAC successor body.

6.14.   While we are satisfied that tribunal doctors, whether they be full members or expert advisors, and second opinion doctors should be provided from the same panel, we are anxious to ensure that those doctors receive the necessary training to enable them adequately to perform their second opinion role and that they be properly monitored in the performance of that role. In our Draft Proposals we suggested that the MHAC successor body should have a part to play here and this met with considerable approval. However, we recommend further consultation on this issue with bodies such as the Council on Tribunals and the Judicial Studies Board when the final shape of the tribunal is agreed.

6.15. At present the SOAD is asked essentially to consider whether the proposed treatment falls within acceptable psychiatric practice. The suggestion in our Draft Proposals that the test be made more rigorous attracted widespread support and we recommend that it be expressed in terms which reflect the requirements of criteria in para 5.95.ii. and 5.95.iii.

6.16. In our Draft Proposals we mentioned the difficulties encountered by SOAD visits out of hours and the need to consult a third professional and suggested the possibility that a non medical member of the team be required to leave a report for the certifying doctor. Having considered the responses received on this we have decided to make no such recommendation. We are satisfied that the need to present a care and treatment plan to the tribunal will itself encourage multi-disciplinary working. We also recommend that independent advocacy be available to patients on the occasion of a second opinion visit in order to help patients to express their views.

6.17. Finally, under the proposed structure the regaining of capacity by a patient may be grounds for discharge from compulsion. We therefore recommend that second opinion doctors be required to contact the tribunal if they believe that the patient now has the capacity to consent to treatment for mental disorder. Such information could provide grounds for the tribunal to review the case of its own motion, see above.

ECT

6.18. In our Draft Proposals we indicated our intention to make the following recommendations:

i   that ECT be never imposed on any patient who retains capacity and is not consenting;

ii   in the case of patients without capacity, whether under a compulsory order or not, ECT cannot be administered without the express approval of the tribunal through its medical member.

iii   that ECT should not be available on the equivalent of section 62.

6.19. These recommendations were designed to take account of views expressed both by those who urged the removal of ECT from the list of treatments which can be imposed in the absence of consent and by those, both clinicians and service users, who felt that ECT can be effective, possibly even life saving.

6.20. The general reaction to these proposals has been very positive, although we appreciate that there is a committed body of opinion for whom only the prohibition of all ECT would be sufficient. We therefore endorse the above recommendations. However, our original proposals were phrased on the assumption that there would be a medical member of the tribunal. If our revised recommendations are accepted the necessary expertise may not be provided by medical members, but by a panel of approved independent doctors. Thus our recommendations in relation to ECT should now be read to require the express approval of such a doctor. In this context, unlike the second opinion context, there would appear to be no reason to insist that this doctor should not have been involved in the original confirmation of the compulsory order. Indeed there might be a distinct advantage in selecting someone with a knowledge of the case.

6.21. We have heard argument to the effect that there may be occasions on which delay might endanger life and thus it would be unwise to remove ECT from the scope of the successor to section 62. In the light of this concern, although we wish to retain our exclusion of ECT from section 62, we recommend that the relevant bodies be consulted further and asked to devise a scheme for emergency prior approval which could be activated with sufficient speed.

Other Controlled Treatments

6.22. In our Draft proposals we suggested that depot medication, polypharmacy and doses above BNF be subjected to the same safeguards as those proposed in relation to ECT. Polypharmacy and doses above BNF were selected on the basis of concern about their safety, while depot medication was thought to require special safeguards on the basis of the duration and 'temporally' irreversible nature of the interference involved.

6.23. On the basis of the responses we have received we remain satisfied that it is appropriate to impose special safeguards on treatments other than ECT. We recommend that an obligation be placed on the Secretary of State to do this by way of statutory instrument and that polypharmacy be included from the outset. Polypharmacy should be defined as the concurrent administration of more than two drugs for mental disorder from the same

BNF class. We also recommend that the new act specify the criteria to be taken into account by the Secretary of State in exercising his/her functions in this regard. We recommend that further consultation be conducted on this issue but suggest that these criteria should include patient safety and duration of impact. In addition we consider that users, pharmacists and pharmacologists have an important contribution to make to the development of guidelines on safe and effective treatments.

Feeding Contrary to the Will of the Patient

6.24. This topic has caused much concern in recent years and the Committee is aware of the need for clarification. The recommendations contained in the Draft Proposals attracted little comment and consequently we are inclined to endorse them.

6.25. The Committee recommends that artificial feeding in the case of a person suffering from a mental disorder be placed in the same category as ECT in the act itself, and that the safeguards be applied whether or not the patient is subject to a compulsory order.

Emergency Treatments

6.26. The Committee is persuaded that there will remain a need to provide for the administration of emergency treatments, under an equivalent of section 62, and has identified several points at which such a power may need to be used, for example, paras 5.30 and 5.38, although under the revised proposals the need to rely on emergency treatments during the period of assessment should be greatly reduced. The Committee is also aware of the concern expressed about the possible over reliance on emergency treatments under current arrangements.

6.27. In our Draft Proposals we expressed our intention to recommend the introduction of safeguards and we asked for views on the form those safeguards might take. As a result of the responses we received we now recommend that care teams be required to keep records of all emergency treatments and the reasons for them. These records should be made available to the MHAC successor body either annually or on the occasion of their visits. The MHAC could then monitor the incidence of emergency treatments both between teams and between trusts. The records should also be made available to the tribunal on the next occasion when the patient's case fell to be considered.

6.28. We recommend that a provision be included in the new act which would authorise the compulsory administration of the minimum treatment (primarily medication) necessary to:

i   save the patient's life; or

ii   to prevent a serious deterioration in his/her condition; or

iii   to alleviate the patient's serious suffering.

6.29. While we are keen to provide the power to treat where the patient is experiencing serious suffering, as at 6.28iii above, we are aware of the ease with which such a criterion can be deemed to be met and we recommend that great care be taken to impose as much objectivity as possible when devising its precise wording. Resort to emergency treatment must be kept to a minimum.

6.30. This provision would not authorise the emergency administration of the specifically controlled treatments mentioned at paras 6.18-25. We recommend that the administration of emergency treatment in order to protect others be dealt with by the Statutory Instrument we describe above at para 3.30.

7. INCAPACITY

7.1.   We have explained the importance we attach to the principles of non-discrimination and patient autonomy and have described how adherence to these principles leads to the elevation of capacity to a central role within any future compulsory mental health structure. The criteria for compulsion which we describe above, at para 5.95, include consideration of the patient's capacity and this innovation received considerable support in the responses we received to the Draft Proposals.   Respondents with a wide variety of experiences of mental health care as professionals, users and carers expressed their approval in principle, and the strength of this support seems to derive from the direct link between capacity and patient autonomy and the fundamental justification for compulsory powers. Many of the responses, however, pointed to the need to develop a very careful definition of the term.

7.2.   The precise meaning of capacity or incapacity will vary according to the context in which it is being applied. Capacity is not a general notion but applies in different forms to different tasks. A person might be said to possess the necessary capacity to write a will for example but not to consent to hazardous treatments, or vice versa. An individual's capacity will also vary according to how much information he or she is given and how much support is made available. Finally an individual's capacity in relation to any one task will vary, both over the years through the natural course of development, and according to the severity of his or her disorder at the time.

7.3.   In our Draft Proposals we advocated a broad model of incapacity which is consistent with the Law Commission's approach set out in their Report on *Mental Incapacity* at para 3.15:

7.4.   *"In the consultation papers we* [the Law Commission] *identified two broad sub-sets within this category [as to the meaning of the phrase "unable to make a decision], one based on inability to understand relevant information and the other* **based on inability to make a "true choice"**. *Although many respondents expressed disquiet about the elusiveness of the concept of 'true choice', there was broad agreement that incapacity cannot in every case be ascribed to an inability to understand information. It may arise from an inability to use or negotiate information which has been understood. In most cases an assessor of capacity will have to consider both the ability to understand information and the ability to use it in exercising choice..."* [emphasis added]

7.5.   We remain convinced that such a model is the most appropriate to apply in the context of decisions relating to treatment for mental disorder. Thus we propose a broad model of incapacity which accepts that a person may lack capacity where, although intellectually able to understand and apply the information, that person nonetheless reaches a judgment which s/he would not have reached in the absence of the disorder. Such a judgment can be said to be primarily the product of the disorder and not to reflect the person's true preferences. Paragraphs 3.16 and 3.17 of the Law Commission's Report capture the essence of what we wish to recommend. Thus a person lacks capacity to consent to care and treatment for mental disorder if at the time when the decision needs to be made the mental disorder is such that, either:

i. **'he or she is unable to understand or retain the information relevant to the decision, including information about the reasonably foreseeable consequences of deciding one way or another or failing to make the decision.' (para 3.16);**

or,

ii. **'he or she is unable to make a decision based on the information relevant to the decision, including information about the reasonably foreseeable consequences of deciding one way or another or failing to make the decision.' (para 3.17)**

7.6.   We are, however, well aware of the anxiety the apparent breadth of the test has caused among both those consulted by the Law Commission and those who responded to our Draft Proposals. These anxieties include a fear that it will be up to doctors alone to decide whether the decision reflects a true choice, that the tendency will be to equate incapacity with failure to agree with the doctor, that incapacity will become indistinguishable from lack of insight, that the test is dangerously subjective and that it will lead to an increased use of compulsion.

7.7.   In view of these very real concerns we need to emphasise the points made in our Draft Proposals:

i   there will be a presumption in favour of capacity;

and,

ii   it will be for the tribunal to decide: if the tribunal is not satisfied that capacity has been lost it will not confirm the compulsion unless the criteria set out in para 5.95.v. are satisfied.

7.8. Further, in order to illustrate how the test might be applied in practice and how it is distinguishable from lack of insight we give some examples below. In general terms there are certain key points to bear in mind when identifying the boundary between a decision taken with capacity and one taken without.

i   To what extent is the decision a 'product' of the disorder? In answering this account should be taken of whether the decision conflicts with the individual's views, previously expressed or demonstrated at a time when s/he had capacity.

ii   Imprudence does not on its own amount to lack of capacity.

iii   It is appropriate to take into account the individual's ability to understand the reasonably foreseeable consequences of a decision.

iv   Capacity is a sliding scale - it may be easier to establish lack of capacity where the consequences of the decision to be taken are more onerous: a patient must have capacity 'commensurate with the gravity of the decision he purported to make' (*Re T* [1992] 2 FCR 861 at 874; *Re MB* [1997] 2 FCR 541 at 549).

Some Examples

7.9. These are given simply to illustrate some of the issues which can arise when considering the boundary between capacity and incapacity. There is no suggestion that lack of capacity is itself sufficient to constitute grounds for compulsion.

i   A patient suffers from a severe depressive illness and believes that all food and medicine is poisoned. He accordingly rejects otherwise beneficial treatment. The patient would appear to lack capacity by virtue of 7.8.i above.

ii   A patient with a long history of domestic difficulties becomes severely depressed. She asserts that her life is no longer tolerable since all the strategies she has evolved to cope with her psychological distress have exhausted her and she can not conceive of any improvement to her situation. She refuses treatment on the grounds that treatment could do nothing to alleviate the source of her distress, it would only mask the symptoms. The patient is likely to retain capacity but the more serious the adverse consequences of her refusal become, the stronger the case for incapacity under 7.8.iii. and 7.8.iv. above.

iii A patient with a mental illness and past experience of medication expresses a preference for a less effective drug than the clinician advises, or no drug at all. He considers the side effects of the clinician's preferred treatment to be less welcome than the symptoms of the illness. The patient is likely to retain capacity despite the presence of mental disorder because the decision would not be the product of that disorder according to 7.8.i. and according to 7.8.ii. 'imprudence' alone would be insufficient.

iv A patient with a long established mental illness in remission begins to become unwell again causing concern to all those who know her. She denies that she is changing and, claiming that she feels perfectly well, refuses the treatment which has been beneficial in the past. The patient is likely to lack capacity on the basis of 7.8.i. and 7.8.iii. above.

v A patient with schizophrenia who is known to respond well to medication is convinced he is well after an initial and incomplete improvement, and refuses medication although he is demonstrably still unwell. The patient is likely to lack capacity on the basis of 7.8.iii. above.

vi A patient with schizophrenia responds well to medication and after an initial improvement says he no longer wishes to take it because he can manage without. He appreciates that his condition may well deteriorate and if it does so he has authorised a friend to re-engage with the mental health services on his behalf. The patient would retain capacity.

vii A patient with anorexia has a dangerously low body weight and refuses to eat. She accepts that her life is at risk but believes that that risk is not imminent since her parents have often told her before that if she does not eat she will die and she is still alive. She says the loss of just a few more pounds will do the trick and then she will feel better. The patient is likely to lack capacity on the basis of 7.8.i., 7.8.iii. and 7.8.iv. above.

7.10. The above examples are designed to illustrate the difficulties and to assist in determining the boundaries between capacity and incapacity in relation to decisions concerning care and treatment for mental disorder. We appreciate that the introduction of capacity as an element in the criteria for admission to compulsion is new and will require extensive training and refinement as experience of applying the concept grows. Words used to describe the criteria for compulsion are bound to contain elements which are susceptible to broad interpretation in order to render those criteria sufficiently flexible to operate in practice. Under the present Act the notion of 'appropriateness' remains open to many different interpretations. However, it is our firm view that capacity, unlike 'appropriateness', has an independent value and meaning the core of which is accepted by all those involved in the operation of mental health legislation: mental health professionals, users, carers and lawyers. In our opinion the introduction and development of the concept of capacity will lead to a more precise and objectively justifiable use of compulsory powers.

7.11. In our Draft Proposals we discussed some specific situations which we considered might require further thought and clarification. While some of these situations have been covered in the examples given above, we feel it necessary to return to the following.

The Patient with a Deteriorating Condition

7.12. As we explained in our Draft Proposals, a person with recurring mental disorder may recover sufficiently to regain capacity, however defined, and may pose insufficient risk to attract compulsion on that basis. Such a person might be discharged from compulsion and would thus be free to refuse medication. If such a person begins to display signs of relapse either a relative or a carer could seek a preliminary assessment (see rights to assessment above, paras 3.22-3.23) or an approved mental health worker or doctor could consider initiating a compulsory assessment. It would then be up to the clinical team to determine whether it was appropriate to seek further authority to compel.

7.13. It is obvious from the responses we have received that clear guidance on this issue is required. The majority of respondents consider it to be appropriate to impose treatment on someone who has a substantial history of relapse coupled with a positive response to treatment. Any suggestion that such a person must be allowed to develop florid symptoms of psychosis before treatment is imposed is rejected on the grounds that it would be counterproductive to delay treatment.

7.14. Under a proper understanding of the boundary between capacity and incapacity we would consider that such a person should be regarded as lacking capacity on the basis of points 7.8.i. and 7.8.iii. above, provided there was a clear history of relapse and positive response to treatment. We would also emphasise the important role of advanced agreements in such cases. It should be the practice of care teams wherever possible to negotiate an agreement with patients which would detail an agreed approach in the case of relapse.

Self Harm

7.15. The dilemmas posed by those who harm themselves have concerned the Committee greatly. In cases where the person lacks capacity through mental disorder the solution is clear, a compulsory order is likely to be appropriate. Whether clinicians would wish to treat compulsorily in such cases is a separate issue.

7.16. The problem for the clinician arises if it becomes clear that the patient does have capacity and rejects the treatment in the full understanding of the consequences. This situation brings into apparently sharp focus the difference in approach described at the outset of this report. For those who wish to maintain a consistent approach to patient autonomy it would be inappropriate to intervene compulsorily in the face of a capable refusal whatever the risk to the patient. By contrast those who take a more pragmatic approach would be prepared to countenance compulsory intervention provided there was a sufficient risk to the patient and there was an effective health intervention available. However, in practice, since there is little evidence that compulsory intervention in cases of persistent self harm is effective this last proviso means that the requirements of para 5.95.v. are unlikely to be met, and the same conclusion may be reached whichever approach to patient autonomy is maintained. Compulsion, in any event, will rarely be the clinically preferred option.

Suicide

7.17. The dilemma here is similar to that described above, but where the threat is of suicide and there is mental disorder the Committee anticipates that most clinicians would regard the patient as lacking capacity, possibly on the basis of 7.8.iv. above. As we suggested in our Draft Proposals, however, there may be cases where the patient clearly retains capacity and still wants to die. Here the whole clinical team faces an impossible dilemma, but it is not a new dilemma and must already confront teams operating under the current structure.

7.18. Again there may be a difference here between those who take a consistent line on patient autonomy and those who adopt the pragmatic approach. The former would not allow compulsory intervention in the face of a clear capable refusal while the latter would, provided there was an effective health intervention available. However, in the face of a persistent and 'capable' desire to die we believe that it is almost impossible to legislate and this view was supported in the responses we received. We therefore endorse the suggestion made in our Draft Proposals that all that can usefully be done is to provide the principles to guide decisions (as articulated in the criteria for compulsion) and to provide a defence to subsequent claims against clinicians who have acted reasonably according to those principles.

Treatment of the Patient with Capacity

7.19. Whichever fundamental approach to patient autonomy is adopted, it is envisaged that in certain circumstances it will be appropriate to impose compulsion on the capable patient. The difference between the two approaches reflected at paras 2.9 and 2.10 above lies in whether or not a threat of serious harm to self is regarded as sufficient grounds for such intervention. However, under both approaches it is essential that an effective health intervention be available. The question is then raised whether it is appropriate to force the patient to accept that health intervention, or whether containment within a therapeutic environment with the offer of treatment is sufficient to guard against the threatened harm.

7.20. Those who advocate containment alone argue that forced treatment is an additional and severe infringement of personal liberty which is not justified on the grounds of harm prevention. While those who favour enforced treatment point to the possible danger to staff and other patients if detained patients are left untreated, and argue that it is inappropriate to detain someone in a health facility and not to require them to accept treatment.

7.21. In our Draft Proposals we described three possible models for dealing with this dilemma:

a) detention without forced treatment,

b) detention and enforced treatment, and

c) detention with no treatment for a period followed by enforced treatment.

7.22. In the responses both (a) and (b) attracted considerable support, reflecting no doubt the basic divergence in fundamental approach. There was less support for model (c).

7.23. Again we feel this dilemma can only be resolved by a moral judgment which it is ultimately for politicians to make. However we do want to emphasise the context of the debate to ensure its practical significance is not over estimated.

7.24. The patients who pose a sufficient degree of risk, whether to themselves or others, to meet the criteria for compulsion and who retain capacity throughout are likely to be patients with personality disorders, not mental illness alone. Before such patients can be made subject to compulsion there must be an effective health intervention available. In the current state of knowledge most, if not all, such interventions in the case of personality disorder are those which require the co-operation of the patient. It is hard to envisage how they can be both forced on the patient and effective. If the patient fails to co-operate both the clinical team and the tribunal may eventually come to the conclusion that continued compulsion is unjustified on the grounds that, although positive clinical measures are available, there is no reasonable likelihood that they will be used to prevent deterioration or secure an improvement in the patient's mental condition.

8. BEST INTERESTS

8.1. The criteria we are recommending for the imposition of a compulsory order require that the proposed care and treatment is in the patient's best interests. 'Best interests' is a phrase in need of definition because its meaning will vary depending on the context.

8.2. Essentially the choice lies between:

i   a notion of best interests which gives priority to the professional opinion of the clinical team as to what would be in the patient's best interests,

and

ii   one which gives priority to the presumed wishes of the patient as far as they are ascertainable.

8.3. While we would recommend 8.2.ii. we appreciate that in cases of longterm incapacity it might be very difficult to ascertain the wishes of the patient in any genuine sense. Nevertheless we consider it essential that an attempt be made to discover the patient's wishes in all cases. Where such an attempt fails we accept that the care team may have to fall back on their professional judgment of what would be in the patient's best interests. This should not, however, be allowed to detract from the general priority to be given to 8.2.ii.

8.4. Within our proposed scheme the question of best interests will finally fall to be determined by the tribunal but it is important to consider the basis on which this judgment must be made in order to provide guidance to clinical teams.

8.5. We have found the Law Commission's proposals very helpful here (paras 3.26-3.37). These proposals emphasise the need to take into account:

i   the ascertainable past and present wishes of the person concerned and the factors that person would consider if able to do so;

ii   the need to permit the person to participate as far as possible or to improve his or her ability to participate;

iii   the views of other people whom it is appropriate and practicable to consult about the person's wishes and feelings and what would be in the person's best interests;

iv   whether the proposed treatment is the least invasive and restrictive alternative.

8.6. The Committee is attracted to these guidelines which emphasise the need to treat the person as an individual whose preferences and wishes must be respected as far as is practicable. In addition we emphasise the need to protect the religious or cultural preferences of the patient as an individual not simply as a member of a religious or cultural group, and to this end we recommend the involvement of the patient's nominated person or advocate in any discussions.

8.7. Finally we emphasise the vital importance of advance agreements in this context. The more mental health practitioners encourage patients to consider and agree in advance the form of care and treatment they would prefer in the event of illness, the easier it will become accurately to identify an individual's best interests.

9. COMMON LAW STATUTE

9.1. Recent case law has served to highlight the complexity of the relationship between common law and statute in the context of both treatment in an emergency and treatment in the case of incapacity. In our Draft Proposals we expressed the view that in the interests of clarity the statutory framework should seek to be as comprehensive as possible. Thus where the statutory framework applies it should be taken to have replaced the common law: in the case of a person with a mental disorder who fulfils the criteria statute must prevail. This view was approved by the vast majority of respondents who commented.

9.2. Nonetheless, the need to provide emergency treatment outside the act may arise however comprehensive the statute: the highly disturbed person who presents to the Accident and Emergency Department of a general hospital, for example. In such circumstances, if the need for treatment is so urgent that it is inappropriate to wait for the statutory emergency procedures to be implemented (described above at para 5.38) common law must continue to provide authority to detain and to treat through the principle of necessity.

9.3. In addition, unless and until a statute exists to cover substitute decision making for those without capacity to consent to health care treatment generally, we wish to retain the common law as the appropriate framework for the provision of treatment for physical disorder in cases where the patient lacks the capacity to consent to such treatment. Treatment for physical disorder should not be provided under the authority of a mental health act and until such time as a comprehensive legislative framework dealing with decision making for incapacitated adults is introduced, the common law must be regarded as the appropriate vehicle. Thus, in order to avoid any doubt, we recommend the inclusion of a provision to make it clear that in relation to those without capacity, decisions concerning treatment for physical disorders should be made by the relevant professionals in accordance with common law principles. In other words those responsible for the treatment of the physical disorder will be permitted to intervene on the basis of necessity, in accordance with their reasonable opinion of what is in the best interests of the patient, and conducting themselves in accordance with *Bolam* principles which fix the standard of care. Where there is doubt as to what is, or is not, in the patient's best interests, in this common law context, then we would expect to see applications being made to the Family Division of the High Court, paras 5.77-78.

9.4. Finally the new mental health legislation would only cover those who clearly fell within its criteria. We are not recommending that all people with a mental disorder requiring treatment who lack the capacity to consent be placed under a compulsory order. We would prefer to retain 'informality' for those patients who offer no objection, however expressed. In respect of these patients we recommend both that the approval and oversight of certain forms of treatment be required, see above, paras 6.18-25 and that the remit of the MHAC successor body be extended to cover them. If the MHAC body was concerned about any individual patient it should have the power to refer that patient's case to the tribunal.

9.5. For such informal patients, therefore, the common law would still provide the essential authority for treatment, save for those forms of treatment for mental disorder referred to above, just as it would in the case of people lacking capacity for reasons other than psychiatric disorder. For the reasons given at para 4.19 we do not consider it appropriate to include this latter group within mental health legislation. We would, however, like to emphasise again the urgent need to provide some statutory framework for substitute decision making and safeguards for such patients. The common law on its own cannot provide sufficient reassurance.

10. Information Sharing

10.1. The failure to share information effectively is frequently referred to in Homicide Inquiry Reports. Its importance is also emphasised in the National Confidential Inquiry Report, *Safer Services* 1999. Perhaps in reflection of this the vast majority of the submissions received by the Committee which referred to the issue advocated the sharing of information, at least between professionals. Many submissions also pointed to a suspicion that some professionals may fail to give sufficiently serious consideration to the information they do receive, particularly from carers.

10.2. The Committee is aware of the complexity of the law in this area and the additional difficulties created by the relevant professional codes of practice and position statements. While we appreciate the need to clarify the position particularly in relation to children and to adults who lack capacity, in our Draft Proposals we expressed our reluctance to recommend the introduction of a specific legislative provision to govern the sharing of information in relation to those who suffer from mental disorder. We expressed a preference instead for the introduction of legislation to clarify confidentiality and disclosure generally in the field of health care services if that is thought necessary.

10.3. Our preferred recommendation that the Code of Practice be expressly required by the act to provide guidance about sharing information in relation to mental health care was widely supported in the responses we received and we therefore endorse it. We also endorse, with some amendments, our earlier suggestions concerning the principles to be reflected in the guidance:

   i   good information is fundamental to the effective care, treatment and support of those with mental health problems;

   ii   sharing information between a service user, carer, nominated person, advocate and professionals is good practice for those people working together to provide care;

   iii   wherever possible information should only be shared with the agreement of the service user;

   iv   where the user lacks capacity to consent to information being shared any sharing should be on the following basis, which we anticipate to be in compliance with article 8 of the ECHR:

   ● the level of need and dependency,

- the nature and degree of assessed risk,

- the relevance of the information to ensuring that the user receives the appropriate level of care, treatment and support;

v   where the user has capacity but disagrees, information sharing will take place only on the following basis:

- there is a serious risk of harm to the user or to others,

- the user will know who has made the decision, and the nature of and reasons for that decision, unless this risks serious harm;

vi   where significant risk to self or others is indicated, information relevant to managing such risk will be shared on a 'need-to-know' basis;

vii   training on the principles governing the sharing of information should be provided to all mental health practitioners.

11. CARERS

11.1. Throughout the above text we have emphasised the important role played by carers and the need both to involve them in planning care and treatment and to offer them all necessary support. Principle viii (para 2.21) of the express principles which we recommend for inclusion in the new act recognises the value of the contribution made by informal carers and the need to help them to care more effectively. In reflection of the carers' need to access care for their friend or relative, sometimes as a matter of urgency, we have recommended the introduction of a right in carers to ask for an assessment. In the course of a compulsory assessment we have recommended that the care team inform and consult the nominated person and where the carer is not the nominated person we recommend that, within the guidelines given above in relation to information sharing, the carer should also be informed and consulted. Further it is essential that before any discharge from hospital or any variation to a community order the carer be consulted and informed, again in compliance with the guidelines relating to information sharing. Before confirming either the variation or the on-going care package we would expect tribunals to check that such consultation had taken place.

12. SAFEGUARDS

Hospital Managers

12.1. We have explained above our reasons for recommending the removal of the managers' right to discharge and, given the characteristics of the proposed framework for compulsion, we now recommend that hospital managers cease to be a feature of future mental health legislation. In making this recommendation we do not wish in any way to imply a lack of appreciation for the important and challenging work undertaken by managers since 1960. The recommendation flows rather from the nature of the changes to the overall framework which we are recommending, in particular the introduction of automatic independent decision making at a much earlier stage and the emphasis placed on advocacy and advance agreements. However, we recommend that further thought be given to the development of other mechanisms to encourage the involvement of local communities in aspects of the provision of mental health care especially where it involves compulsion.

Second Opinion Appointed Doctors

12.2. Under the proposed framework for compulsion there would be no requirement for second opinion appointed doctors (SOADs) as defined and deployed under the current Act. The alternative structure is described in Chapter 6.

Training and Approval

12.3. According to the Committee's proposals a number of different professionals will be empowered to act under the new legislation. For reasons set out elsewhere (para 5.63) we recommend that a statutory obligation to train its own members be placed on the tribunal. In relation to other individuals empowered under the new act, those assessing for admission to compulsory assessment 5.10 –5.16 for example, and the clinical supervisor para 5.34, we recommend that there be a requirement to receive accredited training and formal approval. There should also be provision for refresher training and re-approval. We recommend that one body, the successor to the MHAC, be charged with accreditation, while responsibility for the provision of training and approval should lie with the employing authorities. Further, the provision of joint training should be regarded as an important aspect of the oblgation to establish joint local arrangements as at para 3.34, and the crucial role played by primary care indicates a need to ensure the appropriate training of G.P.s.

12.4. It is certainly not for this Committee to prescribe the length or content of the training and education required for approval under the new act, that will depend on a number of factors including professional qualification and experience. However, the Committee does recommend that the approval and re-approval process include some form of appraisal of relevant professional knowledge, including knowledge of mental health legislation and the Code of Practice and awareness of the principles which underpin them. The re-approval process should also include a requirement that participants provide evidence of their experience in implementing the act.

The Mental Health Act Commission

12.5. In the submissions received in response to Key Themes there was significant support for the extension of the role of the MHAC. In what follows we describe our recommendations in this regard, taking into account the response to our Draft Proposals. We do, however, recognise that if these recommendations are implemented the structure and organisation of the new body may have to be radically different to that of the current MHAC.

12.6. In reaching these recommendations we have paid particular attention to the fact that the field of mental health care is significantly different from other areas of health care in its use of compulsion. We have also noted the emerging quality and performance framework for health and social services and have taken into account the wide range of professionals and agencies in health, social care, criminal justice and other fields with an interest in the delivery of mental health care and the operation of mental health legislation.

12.7. The new successor body to the MHAC which we recommend will provide an important additional safeguard for patients in its role as a guardian of the interests of individual patients. The primary focus of the new body will be towards individual care and treatment and, while the primary duty will be to those patients under compulsion, the new body will also have responsibilities in relation to the care and treatment provided to informal patients.

12.8. We now recommend the continuation of a body such as the MHAC to meet the following needs and to have the following responsibilities:

i   to monitor the treatment and care of all patients with mental disorder in hospital and mental nursing homes and of all those under compulsion in the community. This recommendation envisages the continuation of the Commission's visiting responsibilities but we are now satisfied that the new body should also be empowered to act more proactively in pursuit of its statutory responsibilities. In particular the new body should have the power to identify specific themes for scrutiny;

ii   to monitor compliance with mental health legislation and the Code of Practice, and to have the power to report breaches to the Secretary of State and a duty to record such breaches in its biennial report together with their outcome;

iii   to have the power to provide legal practice advice about the implementation of compulsory powers;

iv   to be involved at the appropriate level (possibly through accreditation) in the provision of the training required of those professionals who wish to operate under the Act and in relation to the training of tribunal members we recommend that the new body be invited to contribute as appropriate;

v   to receive notification of all admissions to, extensions of and discharges from compulsion, together with a responsibility to monitor, analyse and publish such data in its biennial report to Parliament;

vi   to have the power to refer a patient's case to the tribunal;

vii   to create working links with all relevant regulatory and other similar bodies and to provide a focus for all agencies and bodies involved in the provision of mental health care;

viii to receive reports of all patients who die while under compulsion and to have the power to investigate;

ix   to have the right to be consulted in relation to the drafting or redrafting of the Code of Practice;

x   to be required to report biennially to Parliament, and to have the power to make special reports.

12.9.   We also note here our recommendations that the remit of the new body be extended to cover informally detained patients in the community, para 14.3, and prisoners awaiting transfer, para 16.10.

12.10. At present the MHAC has a statutory complaints remit. We now recommend that this specific remit be replaced by a general power to investigate such matters as it sees fit which fall within its jurisdiction, whether or not they arise from a complaint, but that in relation to complaints it should have regard to the availability of alternative complaints procedures.

12.11. The current MHAC is a special health authority which undertakes its statutory responsibilities on behalf of the Secretary of State through whom it reports to Parliament. In our Draft Proposals we recommended that the new body should be fully independent of state agencies and of government, and that it be answerable directly to Parliament, possibly through the Health Select Committee, to whom it should make its biennial report. This recommendation was strongly supported and we now endorse it.

Advance Agreements about Care

12.12. In our Draft Proposals we canvassed the possibility of recommending that, in reflection of the principle of patient autonomy, advance directives be given statutory recognition in any future mental health legislation. We suggested that advance directives be recognised as expressions of a patient's capable wishes, and that they be allowed to prevail in the same circumstances under the new act as those in which the wishes of the patient with capacity at the time would be allowed to prevail. Although the proposals attracted considerable support, we now acknowledge that it would be difficult to accord statutory recognition only to directives about care and treatment for mental disorder.

12.13. However, we recognise that certain forms of advance healthcare statement already have full effect in common law, although they have yet to be recognised by act of Parliament. We therefore recommend that the necessary provisions be introduced in statute and complemented by the Code of Practice, to ensure both that the creation of an 'advance agreement about care' is routinely considered by care teams and patients and that when created these agreements would have sufficient formality to be regarded as proper statements of a patient's capable wishes. In essence an advance agreement about care would represent the written outcome of a discussion between a patient, with the necessary capacity, and his or her care team. It would address the patient's treatment preference (if any) in relation to any possible future care and treatment for mental disorder, and it would have to be taken into account as a capable expression of the patient's preferences should treatment become necessary at a future point when the patient has lost capacity.

12.14. We are firmly of the view that the creation and recognition of such agreements would greatly assist in the promotion of informal and certainly consensual care. Patients and care teams would become used to negotiating an agreed package of care to be implemented in the case of relapse.

12.15. Accordingly, we recommend that an obligation be placed on the care team to provide all patients, prior to discharge from compulsion, with information about and assistance with the creation of an advance agreement about care. We further recommend that any discussion concerning an advance agreement should involve the patient's nominated person and/or advocate and, with the patient's consent, any relevant carer. The details of the form to be taken by advance agreements and the matters they might include should be contained in the Code of Practice, which should set out guidance as to how advance agreements can be constructed in such a way as to achieve recognition in law.

Nearest Relatives and Advocacy

12.16. The recommendations in the Draft Proposals about nearest relatives received some support, especially in relation to the proposed changes to the current statutory specification of nearest relative. However, it is now clear to us that we must differentiate more sharply between our recommendations in relation to nearest relatives, advocacy and carers.

Nearest Relatives and Nominated Persons

12.17. The Committee accepts that there is a continuing need for a figure with some of the entitlements and obligations currently given to the nearest relative. However, in the context of our proposal to introduce greater independent decision making into the compulsion process, we have concluded that the powers of such a statutory figure should be reduced. While the identification of such a person should be accorded the highest priority, the consequences of there not being such a person at any particular stage in the compulsion process should not be sufficient to interfere with the validity of that process.

12.18. We recommend that future legislation should make no reference to the nearest relative. Instead the new act should make provision for the identification of a 'nominated person' and accord that figure certain rights and responsibilities.

12.19. The nominated person should not have the powers of application and discharge currently possessed by the nearest relative. Such a person would, however, receive notification of the patient's compulsion and there would be an obligation to consult such a person during the course of a compulsory assessment and prior to either discharge or substantial variation of the order. There would be no absolute obligation to consult prior to the imposition of compulsory assessment.

12.20. The nominated person would be empowered to apply to the tribunal for a discharge on behalf of the patient, and would have the right, if the patient so wished, to attend any tribunal hearing and to be present at any consultation with a tribunal approved doctor with a view to authorising treatment.

12.21. In light of the widespread criticism of the current statutory specification we recommend that where possible the patient should be empowered to appoint their own nominated person. Such a person might be a relative, friend, carer or an advocate. In the context of our proposals concerning advance agreements about care we strongly recommend that the identification of a nominated person should be a central focus, especially for those patients who are likely to be assessed for compulsion on future occasions.

12.22. It is possible that a patient who becomes subject to compulsory assessment procedures for the first time will not have an identified nominated person. In cases where the patient is unable to nominate we have considered whether any future mental health legislation should incorporate a fall-back statutory table, of the type to be found at section 26 of the current Act, in order to provide for the absence. However, in the light of the greater regulation of the compulsion process which we recommend, we have concluded that such provision is unnecessary, particularly in relation to the imposition of compulsory assessment. Instead we recommend that the care team be required to encourage the patient to identify a nominated person as soon as possible. If the patient remains unable to do so then the absence of such a person should be addressed by the tribunal when it considers the confirmation of the compulsory order. The tribunal should then appoint a nominated person to continue in that role until either the nominated person or the patient applies to the tribunal for a change. In making such appointments the tribunal would be required to take into account the ability of the individual to undertake the necessary responsibilities in the circumstances of each case. In the case of patients with capacity who choose not to appoint a nominated person we do not recommend that the tribunal be empowered to make such an appointment.

12.23. We accept that it will be necessary for the legislation to provide for the replacement of a nominated person. One of the major criticisms of the displacement powers in the current Act is the apparent inability to remove a nearest relative on the grounds that he or she is abusing the patient. We accept that any such provisions would have to be very carefully drafted and should be confined to circumstances where the nominated person was either abusing the patient, purporting to act in ways that exceeded his or her powers or, in undertaking his or her responsibilities was behaving in such a way as to endanger the patient. We recommend that displacement should be a matter for the tribunal which, if it displaced the nominated person, would be obliged to facilitate a replacement.

Advocacy

12.24. The significance given to advocacy in our Draft Report attracted wide support but there were those who urged very strongly that a statutory right to advocacy should be introduced. We are now satisfied that access to independent advocacy will be vital if the fundamental principles which underlie our recommendations are to be achieved. Our whole scheme is designed wherever possible to facilitate informal and consensual care and to that end to encourage the participation of patients in decisions about their care, whether during a period of disorder or in anticipation of relapse into disorder. We recognise that in order to participate in this way patients must be provided with the relevant information in an accessible form and we have therefore recommended the introduction of a right to this information. We have also recommended that patients be entitled to identify their own nominated person. However, there may be occasions, in relation to the identification of the patient's best interests for example, on which a patient needs the support and advice of someone independent of the detaining authority but familiar with the mental health services and the provisions of the act, and who is prepared to speak to the care team on the patient's behalf. An advocate would be ideally suited to perform this role and could indeed provide help and advice to the nominated person as well.

12.25. In our Draft Proposals we expressed concern about the resources required if a statutory right to advocacy were to be introduced for all patients under compulsion. However, creating a right of access to an advocate for those subject to compulsion does not necessarily imply the need for directly state funded services. There are many different models of advocacy.

12.26. We therefore recommend:

    i   that a duty be imposed on the Secretary of State to ensure, by whatever means he thinks fit, the adequate provision of advocacy for those subject to compulsion;

    ii   that advocates be given specific rights of access to patients under compulsion;

    iii   that relevant authorities have a duty to respond to a patient's advocate;

    iv   that a statutory right to advocacy be created at the earliest opportunity.

12.27. We appreciate the fundamental principles of advocacy, in particular the primary focus given by the advocate to representing the wishes of the patient and the independence of the advocate from the service provider, and we would wish to see these safeguarded. However, we also recognise that a regulatory framework will be essential in order to ensure proper training and high standards. There will, for example, have to be provision for the removal of an advocate in certain exceptional circumstances. We have not had the opportunity to consult adequately on the shape this regulation should take and we recommend that the necessary consultation be undertaken as soon as possible.

Protection from Responsibility for Acts Done in Pursuance of Statute

12.28. In response to its Key Themes document the Committee received few comments on the desirability, or otherwise, of including within any future mental health legislation a provision similar to section 139 of the 1983 Act. Sometimes called the 'staff protection clause' this section places additional procedural and substantive requirements on those proposing to bring certain legal actions against people in respect 'of any act purporting to be done in pursuance of this [1983] Act'.

12.29. In part, this provision would appear to be based on a perception that mental health patients are likely to make frivolous claims. The Committee is unaware of any evidence to support this and regards the provision as being in breach of its fundamental principle of non-discrimination on the grounds of mental health. It recommends that no equivalent to section 139 be contained within future legislation. The more rigorous court control of proceedings, explicit in the Civil Procedure Rules 1999, will in any event provide adequate protection for staff and professionals when faced with vexatious or frivolous claims.

Special Offences

12.30. The Committee is acutely conscious of the vulnerability of those subject to compulsion. It is also keen to protect patients from any unauthorised deprivation of rights and to encourage the maintenance of the highest standards. It therefore wishes to see special offences retained within any new legislation. In particular, the principles underlying section 126 (forgery, false statements etc.) and section 127 (Ill-treatment of patients) of the 1983 Act will remain relevant within any new structure of compulsion, whether in hospital or outside. The Committee recommends that the spirit of these two sections be retained with the language modernised and specific reference added to the sexual abuse of patients.

13. Children

13.1. There appears to be general agreement that the law relating to the treatment of children suffering from mental disorder is in need of clarification. The current multiplicity of legal provision creates a climate of uncertainty, professionals are unsure of their authority and of the legal and ethical entitlements of the children in their care. Ultimately a single framework for the treatment of children without consent is required. A clear majority of those submissions to Key Themes which dealt with the problems relating to children felt that children should be included within mental health legislation. The need to provide clarity and safeguards outweighed the dangers of stigmatisation.

13.2. In our Draft Proposals we expressed our agreement with that view and our intention to recommend that children continue to be covered by the provisions of mental health legislation. We also recognised the need to clarify the issue of capacity and suggested a threshold of 16 years for the presumption of capacity to make treatment decisions i.e. to both accept and refuse treatment. In cases where the clinical team considers the young person of 16 and over to lack capacity it would be necessary, as with adults, to receive tribunal approval of that judgment. At any such hearing we suggested that the young person be represented by a specially trained litigation friend. We were clear that we did not wish to see parents continuing to take responsibility for the admission of 16 and 17 year olds to compulsion.

13.3. In the case of children under 16 we suggested that parents retain the power of substitute decision making, but in the case of children from 10 to 16 there be a rebuttable presumption of capacity. In cases of conflict we envisaged that the professionals would be empowered to override parental consent with the child's interests being represented by a litigation friend.

13.4. The response received on these issues was extremely supportive and we now wish to endorse the recommendations we made. Finally we recommend that children subjected to compulsion under the new act be entitled to accommodation within an environment which is appropriate to their age. This recommendation received overwhelming support reflecting our own desire to ensure that children are not inappropriately detained on adult wards.

14. BOURNEWOOD

14.1. At several points in the above discussion we have referred to the need to create a framework specifically designed to meet the needs of those who suffer from longterm incapacity for whatever reason, and thus to fill the legislative gap revealed in the *Bournewood* case. In our Draft Proposals we expressed the intention to make recommendations concerning the principles which might be reflected in such a framework and we asked for views on what those principles might include.

14.2. Unfortunately we have been unable to match that intention. At the time of our Draft Proposals we had still anticipated that the government would be pursuing legislation following from *Who Decides?* and we had assumed that it would be possible to expand that legislation in order to provide the necessary framework. It is now clear that no legislative initiative is likely in the near future. As we have explained above, we would consider it most inappropriate to see compulsion under any new mental health act as a partial answer to the gap revealed by *Bournewood*. A comprehensive statutory framework for substitute decision making is required, see discussion at para 4.19 above. At a minimum this would need to address the issues raised both by the Law Commission in their Report *Mental Incapacity* and by the Lord Chancellor's Department in *Who Decides?* But it would also have to provide for the recognition and review of detention, which could in practice take place in any number of settings. It is a considerable task which must be addressed with some urgency, not least because the absence of adequate safeguards renders the government vulnerable under the provisions of the ECHR and thus the Human Rights Act.

14.3. Within the timetable given to us we would have been quite unable to do justice to the issues and so can do no more than stress the urgency of the problem and repeat, with some amendment, the principles we outlined in our Draft Proposals as those which should be reflected in the new framework:

    i   the creation of an appropriate structure for substitute decision making, which must include adequate provision for the recognition and review of detention;

    ii   the provision of advocacy;

    iii   the extension of the remit of the successor body to the MHAC to cover incapacitated adults wherever they are detained;

iv   the introduction of the same safeguards with regard to the approval of treatment for mental disorder as would apply to those under compulsion under the new mental health act;

v   the publication, after appropriate consultation, of a specific Code of Practice;

vi   the adoption of a coherent approach to longterm incapacity in the national service frameworks;

vii   the recognition of the role and value of carers, and the adoption of a principle similar to that recommended at para 2.21.viii.

15. OFFENDERS

15.1. Up to this point the recommendations have dealt primarily with people who might enter compulsion via the civil route. We are very conscious of the fact that where mental health problems are revealed in the context of offending, especially offending of a serious nature, the difficulties involved in identifying the appropriate balance between occasionally conflicting principles and aims are particularly acute. Moreover, we note that aspects of this complex area have already been addressed by both the Reed Committee in 1992 and the Law Commission in its Draft Criminal Code, which largely reproduces the recommendations of the Butler Committee on mental condition defences (*Report of the Committee on Mentally Abnormal Offenders*, H.M.S.O, 1975).

15.2. In embarking on our overall task we decided that we would first try to establish the principles which should apply to civil patients and would then consider the extent to which those principles might require adjustment to meet the needs of people who enter mental health care via the criminal justice process. In the event our progress in this latter area has been limited.

15.3. In the first place, as we described in our Draft Proposals, the existing legislative landscape is highly complex and in need of rationalisation. Reform of the Criminal Procedure (Insanity and Unfitness to Plead) Act in 1991, the provisions in the Police and Criminal Evidence Act 1984 dealing with the position of those suspected to be mentally disordered offenders, and the most recent changes in sentencing options introduced by the Crime (Sentences) Act 1997 have, amongst other legislative and policy initiatives, produced a complex and not wholly coherent system within which the provisions of Part III of the 1983 Act are required to operate.

15.4. Secondly, during the course of our deliberations there has been uncertainty concerning the precise nature of the government's proposals in respect of severe personality disorder. We have not therefore been in a position to consider our recommendations against a clear picture of the government's intentions in this important area.

15.5. Thirdly we are convinced that the major issues of principle and policy which are raised by the question of how best to deal with mentally disordered offenders deserve far more rigorous and comprehensive consultation and consideration than we have had the time or resources to provide. We refer:

i   to the interface between patient autonomy and public safety;

ii   to the debate concerning how best public safety can be achieved;

iii   to the question of the extent, if any, to which people with mental disorder who come to the attention of the authorities via the criminal justice system should be treated differently from those who enter through the civil route; and

iv   to the extent to which a mental health act should seek to remedy the deficiencies in our mental condition defences.

15.6.   Finally, we were established to advise ministers within the Department of Health. The issues relating to mentally disordered offenders impact most directly on the responsibilities of the Home Office. While we have received considerable support from officials within the Home Office we have not been in a position to conduct the thorough review of Part III of the existing Act which we consider to be essential. We are convinced that such a review is urgently required and, in order to enhance the prospect of coherent legislative reform, we recommend that some other, independent, body be charged explicitly with undertaking it in the light of our recommendations. We also reiterate the recommendation in our Draft Proposals that the raft of legislative provisions which impact on mentally disordered offenders be rationalised and brought together, in much the same way as we are recommending a coherent structure for non-compulsory community based services.

15.7.   In addition we make the following recommendations concerning issues of principle and offer some specific comments in relation to the shape of future legislation.

Issues of Principle

15.8.   We urge that the humanitarian flavour of Part III of the existing Act be sustained and strengthened wherever possible. We recognise that such a humanitarian approach which gives priority to the provision of treatment rather than punishment is easier to maintain where offenders either have serious mental disorders, or their disorders are manifestly linked to their offending, or they have offended at the less serious end of the criminal spectrum. While we accept that the high incidence of various forms of personality disorder within the prison population is probably to be expected, we are concerned by the number of offenders with obvious mental illness who are still detained within prison. Many respondents to our Draft Proposals pointed to the continuing delays in effecting a transfer.

15.9. Wherever offenders, whether convicted or unconvicted, satisfy our recommended criteria for a compulsory order by reason of their lack of capacity, they should be dealt with primarily according to their health needs. Established or suspected offending should not become a reason for denying disordered people access to suitable health facilities.

15.10. The provision of care and treatment for mental disorder in relation to offenders, or suspected offenders, should be dealt with under the same legislation as that which applies to non-offenders. Involvement with the criminal justice process should not alter the basis on which an individual enjoys access to health care.

15.11. Hospitals should not be used and health professionals should not be required to detain offenders who are persistently unwilling to engage in treatment or who are untreatable. For those who pose a serious risk to others and who have offended but who are untreatable, either through their own reluctance to accept treatment or for other reasons, the criminal justice system must provide the appropriate retribution and/or incapacitation. In the context of non-offender patients we discussed the dilemmas posed by those who present serious risks, but nonetheless retain capacity and refuse treatment. We expressed the view that the majority of such patients would be suffering from personality disorders rather than mental illness on its own. In the context of the civil provisions this poses particular difficulties. On the one hand there may be no health benefit in detaining such a capable but unco-operative patient in hospital because the effectiveness of any available intervention would depend on his or her co-operation. On the other hand detention in hospital may appear to be the only available answer to the question of public safety, however inappropriate such detention might be. In the context of offender patients the dilemma is not so stark. If offender patients render themselves effectively untreatable by reason of their refusal to co-operate, a penal order may be imposed, subject to the power to transfer the individual into health care should circumstances change.

The Health Order

15.12. We are agreed that the possibility of a hospital disposal must remain available to the sentencing court. We are also aware of the fact that the present system can give rise to injustice through offender patients being detained for periods either in excess of those which would be proportionate to their offences or for shorter periods than the principle of proportionality would demand. However, given the idiosyncratic nature of the current mental condition defences, we do not consider it possible to construct a system which maintains an entirely consistent balance between treatment and punishment. Rather we have tried to outline a scheme which would reflect the principles described above while at the same time would pay sufficient regard to the need to protect public safety.

15.13. We endorse the recommendation in our Draft Proposals that the trial court be empowered to impose a health order where the entry criteria proposed in relation to civil patients are established and the offender patient lacks capacity. Such an order could apply either in hospital or in the community and would last, in the first instance for a maximum of 6 months. In order to provide access to the necessary expertise when making such an order, we recommend that the trial court be empowered to call on the panel of independent doctors appointed to advise the tribunal (see para 5.68). After the initial imposition of the order by the trial court the offender patient would fall to be dealt with, as at present, as if s/he had entered the system through the civil route, unless the trial court imposed a restriction order, see below.

15.14. As we indicated above, we see the position of the offender with a mental disorder who retains capacity and but fulfils the civil criterion described at para 5.95.v., as more difficult. We do not anticipate that all such offenders would fulfil the criteria envisaged for entry to the government's proposed scheme for severe personality disorders and we would, therefore, like to ensure that wherever possible a health order would be available for such offenders provided their disorder can benefit from a health intervention. To leave in prison offenders who could benefit from treatment would not be productive of public safety. However, in the vast majority of cases where capacity is retained the effectiveness of any health intervention will depend on the co-operation of the offender. Thus, while we understand the apparent contradiction involved in the notion of a criminal court order with consent, we would emphasise the need to take account of the relevance of co-operation to the successful outcome of any health intervention in these cases. One solution may be a greater use of interim health orders. The unco-operative or otherwise untreatable offender patient could then be identified and returned to court for the imposition of a penal sentence.

15.15. As we explained in our Draft Proposals we are concerned about the position of the person with a learning disability who is convicted of a criminal offence. If specific legislation is eventually introduced to provide an appropriate decision making structure for those with learning disabilities we are anxious to ensure that a health option remain available to the criminal courts whatever the criteria for civil admission. Ideally, after the creation of a comprehensive framework for those with longterm incapacity, we would wish to see an option open to the trial court which, in substitution for a criminal sentence, would allow transfer into the incapacity legislative scheme.

15.16.   Finally, we would like to recommend the greater use of transfer provisions where offenders meet the civil criteria for admission to compulsion. To deny offenders access to appropriate health care is to discriminate unjustifiably. We deal with the question of prisoners' access to mental health services below.

The Restriction Order

15.17.   At present it is open to the trial court to impose a restriction order where it is thought necessary to protect the public from serious harm. We regard this power to identify high risk cases as an essential safeguard and would recommend its continuance. In our Draft Proposals we expressed the intention to recommend that a restriction order should only arise on the suggestion of the court itself. We were anxious to ensure that restriction orders were only made on the basis of a clear and objective risk assessment. In the light of the responses to this particular recommendation we realise that it might not be practical to insist that the initiative must always lie with the court. Instead we would recommend the introduction of a requirement that a special risk assessment be conducted before any such order is imposed. This would enable the offender, the clinical team and any subsequent tribunal to understand the reasoning which lay behind the imposition of the order.

15.18.   At present the restriction order carries two significant implications.

The Role of the Home Office

15.19.   A restriction order engages the supervision of a specialised division of the Home Office. All recommendations regarding a restricted patient's transfer, leave of absence etc must acquire the Home Secretary's approval. Only discharge can be ordered against the Home Secretary's advice by the MHRT.

15.20.   While we appreciate both the Home Secretary's proper interest in matters of public safety and the absolute need to protect the public from those patients who pose a real threat of violence, we cannot recommend that the current structure be continued unchanged.

15.21. In the first place, since it is now accepted, and indeed demanded by the Human Rights Act, that an individual subject to detention on the grounds of his or her mental disorder must have the right to test the legality of that detention before an independent 'court', we cannot condone a system which leaves vital preliminary decisions exclusively in the hands of a member of the government. We therefore recommend that the tribunal's power be expanded to include decisions relating to leave of absence from hospital and transfer between hospitals. Trial leave and transfer to conditions of lower security are almost invariably required before the discharge of a 'dangerous' patient can safely be considered. They are essential precursors to discharge and as such they should lie not solely in the hands of a government minister, however well advised, but with an independent judicial body. Control of the exercise of ministerial discretion by way of judicial review is no substitute.

15.22. Secondly we do not consider that the present system makes the best use of the expertise which has built up within the Home Office. The Home Office is in a unique position at present both to monitor overall trends and to maintain long term knowledge of the progress of individual patients. Such expertise should be made available to the tribunals more effectively than it is at present. The MHRTs currently provide the main mechanism for the discharge of restricted patients, approximately 150 conditional discharges are directed by the tribunals each year compared to 30 by the Home Secretary. It is therefore particularly important that they have as full information as possible from the Home Office. However, since tribunals currently expect the Home Office, rule 6, statement (Mental Health Review Tribunal Rules 1983) to be adverse to the patient, they tend, as we understand it, to attach less significance to it than they otherwise might. We would like to encourage a system in which Home Office knowledge and expertise was made more readily available to the tribunal by way of a full report supported by the provision of oral evidence where necessary. Tribunals would then be able to reach their decisions in the light of more comprehensive evidence. In particular the Home Office report could be used where appropriate to present evidence concerning the views and experience of the victim or the victim's family.

15.23. We would therefore like to see the removal of the Home Secretary's exclusive power to authorise transfer and leave in individual cases, but at the same time we would urge the preservation of the knowledge and experience currently available within the Home Office. Under the new structure the Home Office would continue to monitor the progress of all restricted patients. It would be available to advise the clinical supervisor should he or she wish to propose any substantial variation to the patient's treatment and care and to advise the tribunal when any question of transfer, leave, variation or discharge was due to be considered. The final decision on all of these issues would rest with the tribunal, which as at present would be specially constitued to hear restricted cases, but the tribunal should be expressly obliged to consult the Home Office before making any such decision. Further the Home Office, as now, should have the right to make representations to the tribunal.

The Conditional Discharge

15.24. The second significant implication of a restriction order at present, and one which attracts almost universal approval in the submissions, is the availability of the conditional discharge. The conditional discharge is seen to be useful for two principal reasons:

i   it provides access to ongoing care after discharge from hospital detention;

ii   it provides a mechanism for supervision and ultimate recall to hospital based primarily on considerations of public safety.

15.25. Under our recommended structure a variety of conditional discharge will be available to all detained patients through the variation of a compulsory order to apply outside hospital. Thus restricted patients would no longer require a conditional discharge in order to achieve 15.24.i. above. Indeed the compulsory order as proposed could be used directly to require co-operation with medication. However, the criteria governing the compulsory order in the community, while properly devised for non-restricted patients, might not be thought to provide sufficient safeguards in the interests of public safety to replicate 15.24.ii. above.

15.26. Thus we recommend the continuation of the power to impose a conditional discharge in the case of restriction order patients. However, we consider that there are problems relating to the way in which the conditional discharge power under the 1983 Act is currently interpreted. In particular we are concerned by the fact that both community supervision and the power of recall can be applied to a discharged patient who is not, at point of discharge, suffering from a mental disorder, a concern shared by the European Court of Human Rights. We recommend that this aspect of the current provisions be seriously reconsidered in terms both of its underlying justification and of its practical relevance once details of the proposals relating to the management of dangerous people with serious personality disorders are known.

Pre-Trial

15.27. We have had little opportunity to consider the reforms necessary to the range of provisions dealing with the diversion of people with mental disorder from the criminal justice system pre-trial. However, we are aware that people are currently remanded into custody effectively in order to receive an assessment of their mental health. In order to avoid this unsuitable outcome we would recommend that the police be encouraged to call the three professionals to the police station for a 'mental health act assessment' to be undertaken there and that an obligation be placed on the relevant authorities to respond promptly. Such a move would be independent of any subsequent decision whether or not to invoke criminal proceedings. As an alternative the police could be given the power to remand an alleged offender into hospital and, given the authorisation of the necessary three professionals, into compulsory assessment. However, we anticipate difficulties here in relation to access to scarce hospital resources and would recommend further consultation if this option is to be pursued.

16. PRISONERS

16.1. In our Draft Proposals we expressed the view that powers to impose compulsory treatment should not be extended to cover those with mental disorder in prison, whether sentenced or on remand. We took this view because we had received evidence from many respondents, including HM Inspectorate of Prisons, that standards within prison health care centres fail to meet those expected of an NHS in-patient unit, and this has most recently been confirmed by HM Chief Inspector's statement that the regime on the psychiatric ward at Wormwood Scrubs 'was barren and impoverished...was entirely unacceptable... The patients' rights to NHS equivalent health care were not being met'(*Wormwood Scrubs: Report of an Unannounced Inspection 8-12 March 1999* Home Office 1999, para 6.46). While we appreciate that prison health care is to be reorganised we cannot assume that standards can be significantly improved in the short, or even, the medium term.

16.2. It therefore remains our view that it would be entirely inappropriate to permit compulsory treatment for mental disorder in prison. The priority must be to ensure that all those with mental disorder of a severity which would attract compulsion outside prison should be transferred to a suitable hospital facility. The fact of imprisonment must not be allowed to deprive the imprisoned of access to suitable health care, whether for mental or for physical disorder. With this principle in mind we make the following outline recommendations.

A Right to Assessment

16.3. We have recommended above the introduction of a right in non-prisoners to an assessment of mental health needs and we now recommend that this right be expressly extended to prisoners. Further, just as we are recommending a right in carers to request an assessment of their friend or relative, so we would recommend a similar right in members of the prison staff and members of the Board of Visitors to request an assessment of an inmate whose mental state gives rise to concern.

16.4. Such an assessment should be by a suitably accredited mental health professional. It would take place in prison and could result in referral of the individual for consideration for a transfer. In any event the person requesting the assessment should be given a written account of its outcome.

Transfer to Hospital

16.5.   At present the Secretary of State has the power to direct the transfer of a prisoner to hospital if satisfied on the evidence of two doctors that the criteria for admission to treatment are met. Under our recommended scheme such decisions about admission to compulsory care and treatment in relation to civil patients are effectively taken by the tribunal and involve consideration of the proposed care and treatment. If such admission decisions in the case of prisoners were merely to be placed in the hands of the Secretary of State, it would be difficult to enable the assessments required prior to the imposition of the order to be completed while the individual was in prison. Instead we would recommend that the Secretary of State, or the governor acting as his delegate, be empowered to direct the transfer to hospital of a prisoner who, on the evidence of three professionals, he has reasonable grounds to believe meets the requirements for a compulsory assessment. In the case of a prisoner further consideration might be given to the identity of the three professionals. It should be open to the Secretary of State to impose restrictions on such a transfer for assessment which would indicate the level of security required.

16.6.   If after assessment in hospital the clinical supervisor considered it appropriate he or she could apply to the tribunal for authority to impose longterm compulsion as if the prisoner-patient had entered the system via the civil route. If, on the other hand, after a full assessment the clinical supervisor did not consider that compulsory care and treatment was appropriate the individual would be returned to prison. Similarly, if the tribunal did not consider that the criteria for a compulsory order were met it would return the prisoner-patient to prison. In appropriate cases the Secretary of State would be empowered to request that the tribunal impose restrictions on any compulsory order it decided to confirm. Such restrictions would place the transferred prisoner in a similar position to the person on whom a restriction order was placed by the crown court.

16.7.   Once the criteria for a compulsory order and/or the criteria for a conditional discharge were no longer met there would be three outcomes available to the tribunal:

i   if the prison sentence had ended the tribunal would discharge the patient completely/absolutely;

ii   if the prison sentence had only a short period to run, the tribunal would end the compulsory order and would discharge the prisoner-patient into the community with appropriate ongoing care;

iii   if a substantial period of the prison sentence remained, the prisoner-patient would have to be returned to prison, but we would urge that appropriate ongoing care be provided. Indeed according to our recommendations in relation to civil patients the prisoner-patient would have a right to such ongoing care.

16.8.   If the criteria for compulsion and/or the criteria for conditional discharge were still met but it was suggested that the individual no longer required hospital care two different outcomes would be available:

i   if restrictions had been imposed the tribunal could order a conditional discharge;

ii   if there were either no restrictions or a conditional discharge was not thought to be necessary, the tribunal could vary the order to take effect in the community.

16.9.   We would not wish to see prisoner-patients who still fulfilled the criteria for compulsion under the mental health act returned to prison.

16.10.   We appreciate that there is concern at present over the delays which occur while prisoners are awaiting transfer and some respondents have suggested that the power of compulsory treatment should be provided in the case of those who are waiting to be transferred. We would be most reluctant to see any such extension because we fear it would serve to reduce still further the sense of urgency with regard to the need to transfer. In taking this view we are aware of the danger that we are merely encouraging resort to treatment 'under the common law'. For this reason we would like to recommend that the remit of the MHAC successor body be extended to cover prisoners both referred for and awaiting transfer to hospital, and that there be a duty to record all administration of medication said to be justified under common law.

Patients under Compulsion in the Community

16.11.   Our recommendations in relation to civil patients would permit a person to be placed under a compulsory order designed to have effect in the community. If while under such an order the patient is detained under criminal justice powers we recommend that there be provision to allow for early transfer into hospital pre-trial. In the absence of such a transfer the compulsory mental health order must be cancelled, it could not be carried into a prison environment.

17. POSTSCRIPT

17.1.   In the course of this report we have endeavoured to propose a framework for new mental health legislation designed to reflect contemporary patterns of care and treatment. In doing so we have covered the essence of most of what is currently dealt with by the Mental Health Act 1983. However, there are certain topics within that Act which we have not been able to consider in the time available: most notably the Management of Property and Affairs of Patients (Part VII) and Removal and Return of Patients Within United Kingdom, Etc (Part VI).

APPENDIX A

MENTAL HEALTH ACT REVIEW

Expert Group Scoping Study: Terms of Reference

Ministers have decided to review the Mental Health Act 1983 and are seeking advice on the degree to which current legislation needs updating to support effective delivery of modern patterns of clinical and social care for people with mental disorder and to ensure that there is a proper balance between safety (both of individuals and the wider community) and the rights of individual patients. Advice should consider deficiencies in the current legislation -both of commission and omission.

Ministers wish to appoint a group of experts to advise them on the scope of the issues to be considered. The group will comprise experts who will be commissioned to consult widely and to advise Ministers on their findings. It will include representatives from the legal profession, and professional groups involved in the delivery of mental health services. Their report will consider specifically:

- policy intentions established in the NHS White Paper, Our Healthier Nation, the Social Services White Paper and related Welsh Office documents to be delivered through the national service framework for mental health in England and through any associated developments in Wales. Advice will be required on legislative changes needed to support compulsory compliance with the treatment programme, where deemed necessary for those patients not formally detained;

- interface issues with other relevant national legislation or proposed legislation;

- implications of recent case law including recommendations made in Inquiry reports;

- views of service providers and users/carers. It will be particularly important to consider the scope for defining the rights of carers and advising on how these might be taken into account in preparing new legislation.

The Group will have available to them information from an extensive programme of research into the working of the current Act.

Ministers are keen to keep closely involved with the process and the group will report progress on a monthly basis.

Resources

There is scope for site visits and the establishment of seminars for taking evidence on specific issues. Members' expenses will be met. Secretariat support will be provided by the NHS Executive's Mental Health Branch.

Timetable

The group will report to Ministers by the end of April 1999 [extended until 15 July 1999].

APPENDIX B

Methodology

1. In order that our Report can be seen in its proper context, we now describe our methodology and list details of all of the activities we undertook. Our timetable has been extremely tight. Whilst we understood and accepted the urgency of our task, meeting the final deadline has meant that all of our work has been carried out under considerable pressure. Although we have done a great deal in a very short time and been ably assisted by our secretariat, it is evident that this pressure has generated significant burdens on all of those organisations and individuals who have had to give up their time, often at short notice, to support and inform us. Our work has benefited enormously from the quality and depth of the submissions we received and from the many face- to-face meetings we held. We would wish to thank all of those who contributed; the text of the Final Report owes much to those who responded to our various requests for help and comment.

2. However, whilst we have consulted widely and tried to be systematic, there has been a fortuitous element to some of our consultations. Similarly, although we have endeavoured to publicise our activities, particularly by establishing a web page and publishing our Draft Report on the Internet, we are aware that some organisations and many individuals, who would have wanted to comment, remained unaware of our existence until it was too late for them to contribute; indeed, even those organisations who were fully primed, nonetheless, felt that our timetable did not permit them to consult as widely with their membership as they would have wished. This is a matter of regret which we hope will be rectified in the further consultation which we are recommending should take place after the publication of our Final Report.

3. It is also proper that we should record the terms of our appointment; all of us have had to fit our work for the Committee, including the writing of the final report, around our regular jobs. For an exercise of this nature and complexity, this is by no means ideal, and we would wish our Report to be read and understood in this light.

4. The main body of the scoping study was divided into five phases. The first entailed gathering evidence to provide us with an understanding of the current situation. At our first meeting in October 1998, we heard about a variety of issues including feedback on the early stages of the research into the use of current legislation, the scope and limitations of legislation and the early findings of the National Service Framework. We

were also provided with extensive information into the background to the current legislation. On this basis we commissioned expert papers from ten individuals on specific topic areas such as human rights, capacity and the justifications for compulsory detention. In order to impose some structure onto what was to become our written consultation exercise, and to ensure that we received comment on all of the major issues involved, we drew up a list of key themes and questions on which we subsequently invited written comment. This is reproduced as our 'Key Themes' document in the Appendices. During November and December we visited ten sites in rural and urban locations across the country and held discussions with a range of individuals around the Key Themes document. During these visits we met, amongst others, service users, carers and voluntary workers, social services senior managers and approved social workers, consultant psychiatrists, general practitioners, service managers, probation and police officers, and nurses, and were thus enabled directly to seek their views on how well the current legislation worked and how it might be improved.

5.   The second phase was the written consultation Key Themes. The document was sent to over 220 organisations and individuals and written submissions invited by a deadline early in January. In response, we received over 250 submissions. The scale of the response made it necessary for us to engage, on a short term basis, a research assistant who analysed the submissions and synthesised the principal issues raised. During this phase we also received many other packs of information from groups and professionals which helped to inform our thinking. We held twelve further meetings to consider the themes in greater detail during December and January. Those involved included key interest groups, such as nursing, carer organisations and organisations representing older people's and children's interests. Since we were very keen to hear the views of service users and carers we held a seminar in January for key organisations to discuss our emerging thoughts on the scope of legislation and what it might aim to do in terms of protections and rights.

6.   The main aim of the third phase of the study was to develop proposals in the light of what we had learned and to ensure that any new legislation had a principled basis. The Committee considered the way in which formal arrangements for compulsory care and treatment might be remodelled and the entitlements and safeguards which should underpin this. During this phase we also benefited from being exposed to the approach adopted to mental health legislation in other jurisdictions; we both discussed the system in Scotland with officials from the Scottish Office and held two day-long seminars in January and March for our

overseas experts. At these we met clinicians and officials from Sweden, Italy, Norway, Netherlands, France, Germany, USA, Canada and New South Wales. Whilst we were grateful for these seminars and to those who came from a considerable distance to assist us, their principal impact was to make us realise how much more there was to be learnt from the experience of other jurisdictions had we had more time.

7. Whilst the Committee held a number of plenary sessions, we also divided ourselves into three small theme groups to address particular parts of the Key Themes document and to consider the responses to it. Each group formulated a work plan for February, March and April. This involved extensive reading, reviewing the submissions and meeting policy officers at the Department of Health, Home Office, Prison Service and Lord Chancellor's Department. We also met representatives from HM Chief Inspector of Prisons and visited three secure hospital sites. The Committee attended a seminar at which the preliminary findings were reported by the researchers commissioned by the Department of Health to study the workings of the current legislation (the final reports are not due until December 1999).

8. The fourth phase was arguably the most demanding since it involved pulling together the various strands of the study. We produced a Draft Report setting out our outline proposals in April 1999. This was circulated, with apologies for a short deadline, to all of those who had responded to the Key Themes or been involved in the earlier phases of the study. Since we were keen to test the workability of the proposals with those in contact with the legislation on a day-to-day basis we organised three seminars in April and May which took place in London, Bristol and Leeds. We are aware that many did not consider the speed of the arrangements or the format ideal. However, we are grateful to all those who participated.

9. This Draft Report produced even more responses than the Key Themes document. Indeed, over 350 submissions were received at this stage. We also held three final meetings to consider in greater detail the case for the new tribunal with the Council on Tribunals, and the implications for health authorities and trusts with the NHS Confederation, and the implications for Part III with the National Association for the Care and Resettlement of Offenders.

10. The final phase involved the consideration of all these responses, the formulation of our final recommendations and the drafting, by our chair, of the final report.

11.   We hope that our programme of work has achieved wide ranging consultation on the relevant issues with those who have had experience of the Mental Health Act, whether as professionals, users, carers or as members of the many voluntary organisations involved in this field. We have also benefited from being able to consult on the workability of our initial proposals. Whilst we would not pretend that this exercise has been either perfect or comprehensive, we do believe that it is the best that could have been achieved in the time permitted.

ANNEX 1

1. MEETINGS OF THE SCOPING STUDY COMMITTEE AND ITS SUB-GROUPS

PLENARY MEETINGS (all Committee members present)

22/23 October 1998
29 October 1998
30 November 1998
8 February 1999
11/12 March 1999
29/30 March 1999
7/8 June 1999
30 June 1999/1 July 1999

SUB-GROUP MEETINGS

Sub-Group 1 x 5 meetings
Sub-Group 2 x 5 meetings
Sub-Group 3 x 5 meetings

2. PAPERS COMMISSIONED BY THE SCOPING STUDY COMMITTEE

A New Mental Health Act: Justification for Compulsory Detention

Professor Philip Bean
Professor of Criminology,
Director, Midlands Centre for Criminology
& Criminal Justice, Loughborough
University.

Psychopathic Disorders

Professor Jeremy Coid
Academic Section of Forensic Psychiatry
John Howard Centre.

The Clinical Operation of an Incapacity Test in Treating Patients for Mental Disorder without their Consent

Dr Nigel Eastman
Department of Psychiatry,
St George's Hospital.

and

Dr Tony Hope
Ethox Institute of Health Services, Oxford.

Human Rights and EU Law

Philip Fennell
Reader in Law,
Cardiff Law School.

–

Entitlement to Services

Nicola Glover
Faculty of Law,
The University of Liverpool.

Paper on Capacity

Professor Michael Gunn
Department of Academic Legal Studies.
The Nottingham Trent University.

Mental Health Legislation & the Children Act

Anthony Harbour
Scott-Moncrieff, Harbour & Sinclair.
Solicitors.

Mentally Abnormal Offenders - Disposal and Criminal Responsibility Issues

Professor Ronnie Mackay
Professor of Criminal Policy and
Mental Health, School of Law,
De Montfort University,
Leicester.

Paper on Confidentiality

Jean McHale
University of Manchester.

Management of Personality Disorder

Professor Peter Tyrer
Professor of Community Psychiatry,
Imperial College School of Medicine,
London.

3. INTERNATIONAL MENTAL HEALTH LAW SEMINARS ARRANGED BY COMMITTEE

Anglophone Seminar

5/3/99

Professor Simon Verdun-Jones,
School of Criminology,
British Columbia, Canada

Professor Nancy Wolf,
King's Fund

Dr Hoult, Consultant Psychiatrist,
New South Wales (now working at
Camden and Islington NHS Trust)

Dr Virginia Hiday,
Department of Sociology,
North Carolina State University

European Seminar

22/1/99

Per Erik Rinsell, Sweden

Dr Theresa Di Fiandra &
Dr Guido Ditta, Italy

Professor George Hoyer, Norway

Ms Tineke E de Boer Stikker &
Ms Mady Samuels, Netherlands

Monsieur Michel Guyader &
Dr Anne-Marie Gallott, France

Herr Dr Ulrich Hoffman, Germany

SITE AND HOSPITAL VISITS, MEETINGS WITH ORGANISATIONS AND GOVERNMENT DEPARTMENTS AND SEMINARS TO CONSIDER COMMITTEE'S OUTLINE PROPOSALS DOCUMENT

SITE VISITS: NOVEMBER/DECEMBER 1998

Date	Location	Attendance
6/11/98	Birmingham	3 Committee members
6/11/98	Salford	3 Committee members
10/11/98	Shropshire	3 Committee members
17/11/98	East Kent-Dover	3 Committee members
18/11/98	Mid Cheshire	2 Committee members
20/11/98	Bexley/Greenwich	2 Committee members and 2 guest service users
23/11/98	Hackney	3 Committee members and 1 guest service user
23/11/98	Sandwell	2 Committee members
27/11/98	Cardiff	2 Committee members
1/12/98	Somerset	3 Committee members

HOSPITAL VISITS: 1999

Date	Hospital	Committee attendance
2/3/99	Rampton Hospital	2 Committee members
16/3/99	Ealing Hospital	3 Committee members
16/3/99	Maudsley Hospital	3 Committee members

MEETINGS WITH ORGANISATIONS

Date	Organisation	Committee attendance
9/12/98	National Schizophrenia Fellowship	2 Committee
10/12/98	Law Society	3 Committee
16/12/98	Sainsbury Centre for Mental Health & Centre for Mental Health Services Development	3 Committee
17/12/98	The Children's Society Young Minds National Children's Bureau	3 Committee
18/12/98	British Medical Association	2 Committee
21/12/98	Royal College of Psychiatrists	2 Committee
22/12/98	MIND	1 Committee
22/12/98	UNISON Royal College of Nursing National Committee of Special Hospitals: Prison Officers Association Forensic Psychiatric Nurses Association Community Psychiatric Nurses Association	2 Committee
22/12/98	National Alliance for Relatives of the Mentally Ill Making Space SANE	2 Committee
5/1/99	Age Concern (England) Alzheimer's Disease Society Help the Aged	2 Committee

15/1/99	Mental Aftercare Association Manic Depression Fellowship MENCAP MIND + MINDlink Survivors Speak Out UK Advocacy Network Voices (NSF group)	4 Committee
20/1/99	Royal College of General Practitioners	4 Committee members
26/4/99	NACRO	3 Committee members
12/5/99	NHS Confederation	1 Committee member

MEETINGS WITH GOVERNMENT DEPARTMENTS AND OTHER OFFICIAL BODIES

Date	Body	Committee attendance
15/1/99	Mental Health Review Tribunal Regional Chairmen	3 Committee
1/2/99	Department of Health (Policy Sections, Children's issues and older people)	3 Committee
9/2/99	Inspectorate of Healthcare in Prisons	4 Committee
12/2/99	Scottish Office	4 Committee
19/2/99	Department of Health (Policy Sections, Quality in NHS and Social Services)	4 Committee

22/2/99	Lord Chancellors Department Department of Health (Policy Section, Learning Disabilities)	4 Committee
22/2/99	Home Office Prison Service	4 Committee
10/6/99	Council on Tribunals	2 Committee members

SEMINARS TO DISCUSS OUTLINE PROPOSALS DOCUMENT

Date	Seminar Venue	Committee attendance
29/4/99	London Voluntary Resource Sector Centre	7 Committee
4/5/99	Grand Hotel, Bristol	6 Committee
5/5/99	Thackray Medical Museum, Leeds	4 Committee

APPENDIX C

MENTAL HEALTH ACT REVIEW PRIVATE FIRST MEETING OF THE SCOPING STUDY REVIEW TEAM THE LEGAL UNDERPINNING OF A SAFE SOUND AND SUPPORTIVE SERVICE

Speech by Mr Paul Boateng – then Parliamentary Under Secretary of State for Health Delivered at first plenary meeting of the Committee, 22 October 1998

Introduction

1   I am delighted to welcome you to the first meeting of the Mental Health Act Scoping Study Review Team. This is an important event. It signals the start of an important process to which the Government attaches considerable priority.

2   You represent a wide range of expertise and experience across the many key interest areas involved which we need to consider.   You are here to provide input from these key areas, not as representatives of organisations from which you come.

3   And let me say at the outset how grateful I am that you have committed yourselves to this important initiative and for your willingness to work within the tight but achievable timescale that we have set. I should like to give particular thanks to Genevra for agreeing to chair the process.

The New Vision

4   Review of Mental Health Legislation is long overdue. The 1983 Mental Health Act has served well for a decade and a half but there is no doubt that it now reflects a bygone age. Modern patterns of treatment and care - particularly the growing realisation of the importance of social care interventions - mean that legislation that is largely about hospital based treatment is now out of date. Modern legislation must recognise the growing importance of life outside institutional settings for those who are mentally ill.

5   But it is not only because of the shift to modern patterns of care that legislation needs changing. It must also support the robust policies which we are putting in place to ensure that services for people who suffer from a mental illness are safe, sound and supportive and that a proper balance is struck between the rights of individuals and the interests of the wider public on the few occasions where these can sometimes seem to conflict.

6 I referred to the need for legislation to underpin our new policy which, although not formally published yet will be announced very soon. And as you are aware, the main themes of our vision are well known, as a consequence of the speech I gave to the first meeting of the National Service Framework External Reference Group on 29 July. The underlying principle is that mental health services should provide safe, sound and supportive mental health and social care for the patient, for the carer and for society as a whole. This is very much a three dimensional approach to providing care. There are three aims:

- to protect the public and provide effective and safe care for those with severe and enduring mental illness;

- to meet the needs of those with mental health problems who can appropriately and safely be managed within primary health and social care

- to promote good mental health in the population and help build healthier neighbourhoods.

7 The need for this new vision arose because Care in the Community had failed, and it had failed for three reasons: it was underfunded, understaffed and lacked a clear and appropriate legislative framework to support it and in consequence it left people without the care and support that they needed.

8 It is clear that a return to the Victorian Asylums is neither appropriate nor desirable.

9 The principle of people living in their own homes or within supportive neighbourhoods where this is practicable, is one which we wholeheartedly support. But Care in the Community has failed to deliver this in a way that is acceptable to any of the three key groups, - the patient, the carer or the wider public.

10 Greater independence for those with a mental illness can only be realistic if the full range of high quality interventions is available to provide proper positive support. And we are determined that central government and those with responsibility for providing services, or making them available should deliver their side of the deal. You will see from our policy statement that we are going to make significant additional resources available to both health and social care services to underpin proper service provision. The policy will also include the setting of national, evidence-based standards

through our Mental Health National Service Framework. This framework
will be the vehicle which will help to eradicate the unacceptable variations
in performance from one area to another that have characterised Care in
the Community. What have been at times sloppily provided local services
will no longer be tolerated.

11   But if there is a responsibility on statutory authorities to ensure the delivery
of quality services to patients through the application of agreed individual
care plans, so there is also, increasingly, a responsibility on individual
patients to comply with their programmes of care. Non compliance can no
longer be an option when appropriate care in appropriate settings is in
place. I have made it clear to the field that this is not negotiable.

12   We now must consider how best to meet the need for necessary measures
for those living outside hospital, as modern treatment and care
arrangements quite rightly enable more people who are mentally ill to live
in the wider community.

13   But let me be absolutely and unequivocally clear on one point about
this.We are not talking about forcibly administering treatment over the
individual's kitchen table. The new arrangements should only require
compliance with treatment *within an appropriate clinical setting* and
therefore may need powers for compulsory conveyance. And of course, just
as there are currently safeguards built into the current legislation governing
detention in hospital, so too must there be safeguards when it comes to
any requirements to comply with treatment programmes for those who are
living in the community. This must not however stand in the way of early
and effective intervention. Your delivery of this central objective will be
critical to the process of our whole programme of reform.

Legislative framework for new millennium

14   What is plain is that this vision of mental health services cannot be wholly
delivered within the current legal framework. It is also clear that there is a
need to start introducing our new policy as soon as we possibly can -
indeed our Joint Priorities Guidance which we published last month makes
the improvement in mental health services a priority with implementation
starting as early as next April. Of course, it is not possible to change the law
that quickly - but we do not have time to spend in years of contemplation.
One of the main purposes that you have been asked to undertake this
scoping study is to kick start the process and to accelerate the thinking
around what the new legislative framework should look like.

15   What we will need to ensure is that the work is done speedily but thoroughly so that we can move to a mental health act which supports patients getting treatment and supervised care, which fits their needs, the needs of those who care for them and the needs of the wider society.

Expectations of Group

16   I recognise, as I am sure you do, that a lot is expected of you. You are being asked to undertake a root and branch review which will consider all the major issues that must be addressed and to make clear recommendations on how to deal with them in legislative terms.

17   It might be helpful if I clarify some of our wishes and expectations in a way that perhaps amplifies some aspects of your terms of reference. I want to start by saying something about the process of your study.

18   Firstly, I want to make it clear how important we regard the role of the user in all of the work we have been doing to develop mental health policy. And although your job is to reflect policy rather than to develop it there are nevertheless areas in which your advice will have direct impact on how services are to work.

19   It is therefore essential that you involve users to a significant extent. There are a number of models and mechanisms to secure user input. I would welcome your advice as to how I and my Department can facilitate this. Nothing should be ruled out in this regard. I am firmly of the opinion that effective service provision can only be delivered if users have played a key part in their design

20   Secondly, of course is the importance of the views of carers. I am delighted that David Shiers has agreed to be a member of the Group. One of the key issues on which I shall want your advice is how we might reflect the rights of carers. In particular, I shall look to you to give advice on their rights to information to be consulted and their rights to initiate action when things go wrong.

21   I am glad to see that Professor Graham Thornicroft is making a presentation to you as part of this seminar. It is most important that you take account of the work that he is undertaking to develop National Service Framework. Here one of the issues is whether there is scope for enshrining aspects of the quality of service provision in the new Act. I should like advice on how this might best be achieved. An integrated approach to law and practice is vital.

22   I will also look to you to provide a very clear steer on how assessment might work in the future. In particular your work will clearly define the pathways for care following assessment or after a period in-patient treatment. One of these should include recommendations on how, for a small minority of patients we must build in a requirement that compliance with agreed treatment plans is not optional.

23   You will also need to consider the functions of the Mental Health Act Commission and consider the need to revise these or to create a successor body which can address the whole issue of service quality whether for detained or informal patients. This recommendation will need to take account of the policy document "A First Class Service: Quality in the NHS.

24   Your report should clearly identify the issues which the emerging legislation should include, and those which need to dovetail with other pieces of legislation or initiatives. This will include clear recommendations on the legislative framework for people who are mentally incapacitated and who also suffer from a mental disorder. Your clear views on what measures are required will be helpful regardless of the legislative vehicle which is to deliver them.

25   Finally, we will of course need to ensure that the new Act is consistent with the European Convention on Human Rights. As a Government we are fully signed up to the Convention and it follows that the rights of the individual that are enshrined within it must be properly reflected in all our legislation not least the new Mental Health Act. I do not expect this to inhibit but rather inform.

26   I recognise that you may not be able to give definitive proposals on all aspects of the new Act although I expect you to do so in many of them and this includes the requirement to comply with treatment in the community. This is not an opportunity to shirk the difficult issues. At the very least we shall want you to identify clear options with a view on how we should move forward.

Concluding remarks

27   Can I conclude by acknowledging that I do not underestimate the task that you have been set And I am grateful to you for the enthusiasm with which you have accepted this challenging opportunity. We must have legislation that will take us into 2000 and beyond.

28   The Act will need to empower us to meet the needs of all three stake holders - we are looking for three dimensional delivery of safe, sound and supportive policies for those who suffer from a mental illness, those who care for them and for society as a whole.

29   On some of the more difficult issues it is important that we are not bogged down by stock responses from the past. You will need to adopt a fresh approach and find innovative solutions, which will address our new policy requirements.

30   I look forward to seeing your report.

Appendix D

KEY THEMES

In order to manage our task within the timetable we have been given we have tried to isolate the key themes which we will need to consider. These are covered in the following sets of questions.

A.   Coverage of legislation

      i)   Who should be included within the scope of any future mental health legislation and how should that group be defined?

          a)   Should it be by reference to the presence of mental disorder? If so how is mental disorder defined? Should a behavioural test be used?

          b)   Should it be by reference to an incapacity test together with harm to self or others?

          c)   Other?

      ii)   Should any of the following be included within the scope of the legislation and if so to what extent?

          a)   People with learning disabilities?

          b)   People suffering from a personality disorder?

          c)   Children?

          d)   Elderly people?

          e)   Offenders?

          f)   Substance abusers?

          g)   Prisoners?

          h)   The vulnerable/compliant patient who could now be subject to the Act but is dealt with on an informal basis, and/or the de facto detained?

          i)   Other?

iii)   Should any groups currently subject to the Act be excluded?

iv)   Should mental health legislation address the issues raised by *Bournewood?* And if so, how?

B.   Ensuring quality of care

i)   How can mental health legislation be used to ensure the provision of high quality care?

    a)   Should the legislation enshrine patients' entitlements to care (which may include assessment) and to treatment?

    b)   Should the legislation enshrine carers' entitlements and if so, to what?

    c)   Should the legislation impose obligations on professionals, providers and other statutory agencies? And if so, what obligations?

    d)   Should a code of practice, or provisions of one, have statutory force?

    e)   Should the legislation cover the registration and regulation of providers?

C.   Compulsory powers

i)   What is/are the justification/s for intervention despite the objections of a capable patient?

ii)   What are the thresholds which must be met before compulsory powers can be used? How can those thresholds be defined by law?

iii)   By whom should the necessary judgments be made? And who should have the necessary authority to order compulsion?

    a)   Doctors?

    b)   Nurses?

    c)   Social workers?

d) Multi-disciplinary teams?

e) An independent tribunal?

f) The courts?

g) Others?

iv) What form should compulsory powers take:

a) to detain in hospital for assessment? for medical treatment?

b) to assess in the community?

c) to ensure compliance with a care programme in the community, which may include medical treatment?

d) other, eg treatment in prison or in alternative specialised facilities?

v) How and by whom should these powers be enforced? What role should the police play?

vi) How do we ensure that a person placed under compulsion retains all remaining civil liberties?

D. Treatment

i) What should be included within compulsory treatment?

ii) What should be excluded from compulsory treatment?

E. Confidentiality and sharing information

i) how can the legislation ensure that information is shared with relevant others?

ii) how can the need to inform be balanced with the patients' right to privacy?

F.   The ending of compulsion

    i)   What limitations should be placed on the duration of the various forms of compulsion?

    ii)   What mechanisms are required for the review of compulsion?

    iii)   What criteria should be used and how should they relate to the initial thresholds for compulsion?

    iv)   What powers should the reviewing bodies possess?

G.   Safeguards

    i)   We have to consider the whole range of safeguards under the present Act, but we would be particularly grateful for your views on:

        a)   the role of managers under the Act

        b)   the role of mental health review tribunals

        c)   the role of second opinion doctors under Part IV of the Act

        d)   the role of the Mental Health Act Commission

        e)   the role of relatives and carers as 'safeguards'

        f)   the obligation to consult, record and inform

        g)   Special offenses

        h)   Safeguards for mental health professionals.

    ii)   Any other safeguards, including but not limited to, advocacy, advanced directives and clinical governance.

H.   The ECHR and the Human Rights Act and other anti-discriminatory legislation.

    i)   Any aspects of protected human rights enshrined in the Convention and the Statute which have not been covered by **A - G**

    ii)   Any mechanism for avoiding direct or indirect discrimination.

APPENDIX E

Laura Able – Ealing User Involvement Project

Adverse Psychiatric Reactions Information Link (APRIL)

Advocacy Now

The Afiya Trust

African Caribbean Peoples Movement

Age Concern

A K Ainsworth – Chairman East Suffolk Advocacy Network

Alcohol Concern

All Wales User and Survivor Network

Alzheimer's Disease Society

Claire Andrews

Professor Louis Appleby – National Confidential Enquiry into Homicide &
Suicide by People with Mental Illness

Richard Appleton – CPN – Rockingham Forest NHS Trust

Approved Social Work Interest Group – North West

Approved Social Worker Co-ordinators Network – Northern Region

Approved Social Workers – Longsight Mental Health Social Work Team

Simon Armson – The Samaritans

Martin Arnold

Ashworth Hospital Authority

Ashworth Patients Council

Asperger Syndrome Action by Parents

Associate Members of the Leeds Community Mental Health NHS Trust Board

Association of Community Health Councils for England and Wales

Association of Directors of Social Services

Association of Directors of Social Services – Mental Health Strategy Group

Association of Residential Mental Care

Lesley Aston

Avon and Somerset Constabulary

Avon and West Wiltshire – Mental Health NHS Trust

Bob Axford

Joy Bailey – Anorexia and Bulimia Care

Estella Baker – University of Leicester

Heide Baldwin – City and Hackney Community Services NHS Trust

Dr Ann Barker – Parole Board

Martin Barkley – Chief Executive – Nottingham Healthcare NHS Trust

Barnsley Metropolitan Borough Council – Social Services Department

Dr Peter Bartlett – School of Law – University of Nottingham

Richard Bartram – Senior Practitioner

Basildon Association for the Mentally Ill (MIND)

BASW

Professor Philip Bean – Department of Social Sciences Loughborough

Kay Beaumont – ASW

Mr R J Bechervaise

Dr Dominic Beer – The Bracton Centre – Oxleas Trust

Steve Benson

James Berry

Tony & Jill Birch

Birmingham City Council – Social Services Department

Black Country Mental Health NHS Trust

Blaenau Empowerment Group

Bournemouth Social Services Department

David Bowles

Dr P Bracken

The Bradford Group

Bradford Metropolitan District Mental Health Forum

Florence Bradshaw

Dr Branford – Director of Pharmacy – Southern Derbyshire Mental Health Trust

Brent Community Health Council

British Institute of Learning Disabilities

British Medical Association

The British Psychological Society

Broadmoor Hospital Authority

Ms D J Brodie

Alan Brooke-Smith

Calderstones NHS Trust

Camden & Islington, Community Health Services NHS Trust

Cardiff and District Community NHS Trust

Carers (Mental Health) Taunton Dean

Carers National Association

Carers Support Group – Stockhill Day Centre Leeds

David Carson

Christopher Cave-Whitley

Central Council for Education and Training in Social Work

Centre for Mental Health Services Development – Kings College London

Centre for the Analysis of Risk in the Community – Leeds Metropolitan University

Audrey Chamberlain – Development & Information Officer Hampshire Users' Bureau

Cheshire Central Community Health Council

Cheshire County Council

Sheila Chesney – MIND – Basildon Association for Mental Health

The Children's Society

J Christopher Jackson – Leeds Social Services Department

James Churchill - Association for Residential Care

The Church of England – Archbishop' Council

Citizen Advocacy Information & Training

Citizens Commission on Human Rights

City of Liverpool – Social Services Directorate

City of Stoke on Trent – Social Services Department

Sylvia Clayton

Penelope Clennel-White – Practice Supervisor

James J Cockburn – Consultant Emeritus
Kingston & District Community NHS Trust

Gordon Barry Codling

Dr John Colgan – Springfield University Hospital

Community Mental Health Forum – Bethlem and Maudsley NHS Trust

Community Mental Health Team Management Association

Community Psychiatric Nurses Association

Community Psychiatric Nurses – East Kent Community NHS Trust

Consultant Psychiatrists – Coventry

Consultant Psychogeriatricians –- Mental Health Services of Salford NHS Trust

Consumer Relations Manager – Nottingham Healthcare NHS Trust

Susan Cooper

Rosemarie Cope – South Birmingham Mental Health NHS Trust

Dr Margaret Cork – Director Mental Health & Learning Disabilities
South Devon Healthcare NHS Trust

Council for Disabled Children

Council on Tribunals

Dr B E Cox

Janet Cresswell

Dave Crighton – The British Psychological Society

Eleanor Dace

Julian D'Allen – Mental Health User Participation Worker for South Somerset

Dartford & Gravesham Advocacy Network

Dr Martin Deahl – Division of Psychiatry – Homerton Hospital

Professor Christine Dean – The Brooklands

Dr Tom Dening

Department of Forensic Psychiatry – Maudsley Institute of Psychiatry

Department of General Psychiatry – St George's Hospital Medical School

Department of Public Mental Health-Imperial College School of Medicine

James de Pury – Worthing Priority Care NHS Trust

Dr Donald Dick

Sally Dickinson – The Magistrates' Association

Disability Policy Division – Department for Education and Employment

Rosie Doy – School of Nursing and Midwifery

Patti Ducie

Ealing, Hammersmith and Fulham NHS Mental Health Trust

Ealing User Involvement Project

East Cheshire NHS Trust

Dr Nigel Eastman – St George's Hospital

ECT Anonymous

Karen Edmunds – GLAD

Paul and Audrey Edwards

Peter Edwards & Co

Elcena Jeffers Foundation

Wendy & Graham Enderby

English National Board for Nursing, Midwifery & Health Visiting

Sue Evans – Pembrokeshire MIND

Exeter Mental Health Service Users Group

Dr Tim Exworthy – Consultant Forensic Psychiatrist – Redford Lodge Hospital

Dr W Falkowski

Dr C F Fear – Severn NHS Trust

George Fernando

Flintshire County Council – Social Services Department

Forensic Clinical Psychology Special Interest Group

42ND STREET – Members Group

Peter Franklin

Stephen Gascoyne – Approved Social Worker - North Yorks Area

David Gladstone

Heather Goldsack – Carers Voice

Peter S Gourlay – Action Against Harmful Interrogation

Greater London Association of Disabled People (GLAD)

Angela Greatley – King's Fund

Christopher Green – Royal College of Nursing

Pat Guinan – The Professional Affairs Board – The British Psychological Society

Esther Hack

Hackney Users Support Group

The Hon Mrs Justice Hale DBE formerly Professor B M Hoggett
Law Commissioner

Keith John Hall

Mrs F E Halsall

Louise Hamilton – Wakefield and Pontefract Community NHS Trust

Hammersmith and Fulham Association for Mental Health

Hampshire and Portsmouth Social Services Emergency Duty Team
Approved Social Workers

Hampshire County Council Social Services Department

Roger Hargreaves

David Ronald Harries

Dr Michael Harris – Medical Director – St Andrew's Hospital

Dr T M Harrison

Mrs S Hartnell-Beavis – Somerset Community Health Council

Dr Michael T Haslam – Chair of Society of Clinical Psychiatrists

Barbara Hatfield – Mental Health Social Research Unit
School Of Psychiatry and Behavioural Sciences – University of Manchester

Dave Hawkins – Senior Practitioner Community Health
Bradford Social Services Department

Lisa Haywood – City and Hackney Mind

J Healy

Dr Nick Hervey on behalf of Southwark Approved Social Workers

Dr. Pearl D J Hettiaratchy

Sally Hextall – Taunton Association for the Homeless

Simon Heyes

Gail Hill

Dr Oscar Hill

Peter Hill

J E Hilman – Department of Health and Social Services

H M Prison Service

Dr Ulrich Hoffman – Ministerium fur Arbeit, Soziales, Gesundheit und Frauen

Dr Frank Holloway – Maudsley Hospital

R G Holt – Solicitor – Godloves

Home Affairs Committee – The Church of England Archbishop's Council

Dr A Horne – Broadmoor Hospital

Hounslow & Spelthorne Community & Mental Health NHS Trust

Michael Howlett – Director – The Zito Trust

Andrew Hughes – Distress Awareness Training Agency

Rob Huitson- MDO Coordinator

Dr Martin Humphreys – Department of Psychiatry – University of Birmingham

Val Imms – Approved Social Worker

Independent Healthcare Association

Inner Cities Initiative Group

David Inskip - ASW West Yorks Area

Institute of Health Studies – University of Plymouth

Institute of Mental Health Act Practitioners

Dr A Inwald

Mrs Elaine Isaacs

Tim Jackson

Philip John Jaquiery

Ginny Jenkins – Action on Elder Abuse

The Jewish Association for the Mentally Ill

Kathy Johnson - Head of Mental Health Services
Kent County Council Social Services Department

Dr Susan J Johnston – Senior Lecturer / Consultant Psychiatrist
(Learning Disabilities) Rampton Hospital Authority / University of Sheffield

Lucy Johnstone – University of the West of England

Caren Jury – South Glamorgan Probation

JUSTICE

The Justices' Clerks' Society

Ramzia Kabbani

Mary Kane – Regional Chairman Mental Health Review Tribunal (Southern and
South and West Region)

Dr A Kellam – Consultant Psychiatrist

Shaun Kemp

Pam Kendall – Approved Social Worker - Conifers Community Mental Health
Service

Dr H G Kennedy – Consultant Forensic Psychiatrist / Clinical Director

Kent Council Social Services Department

Kent Forensic Psychiatry Service

Rose Kernahan – ASW West Yorks Area

Kingston & District Community Health Trust

G D T Lane – The League of Friends of Mental Health in North Gwent

Dr G E Langley

Dr John Langton – Shropshire's Community & Mental Health Services NHS Trust

The Law Commission

Frances Lawman F.S.W. – Making Space

The Law Society

Learning Disabilities Team – Harrow and Hillingdon NHS Trust

'The Leeds Initiative' – School of Sociology & Policy – University of Leeds

Leeds Irish Health & Homes

Leeds Mental Health Advocacy Group

Leeds Metropolitan University

Hilary E Leigh

Lewisham (Mental Health) Users Forum

LIBERTY – The National Council for Civil Liberty

Lincolnshire County Council – Social Services Directorate

Local Government Association – Health & Social Affairs

Dr Stephen Logsdail – Frenchay Hospital

London Borough of Lambeth – ASW Forum
Department of Social Services

Dr N Longhurst

Lord Chancellor's Department

Dr Simon Lovestone – Old Age Psychiatry
Institute of Psychiatry

J Lynch

Professor R D Mackay – School of Law – De Montfort University Leicester

The Magistrates' Association

Maidstone Community Health Council

Making Space

Malinsgate Police Station – West Mercia Constabulary

Manic Depression Fellowship

Kathy Manovitch – ASW West Yorks Area

Mr E.A. Marsh

Mary McCann

Robert McLean – North West Approved Social Work Interest Group

Lady Margaret McNair – Citizens Commission on Human Rights

Medical Staff Committee – Northumberland Mental Health NHS Trust

Mencap

Mental Aftercare Association (MACA)

Mental Health Act Commission

Mental Health Commission for Northern Ireland

Mental Health Community Forum – The Bethlem & Maudsley NHS Trust

Mental Health Foundation

Mental Health Services of Salford NHS Trust

Mental Health Teaching Team – Faculty of Human Sciences
Institute of Health Studies – University of Plymouth

Mental Illness Concerns All (MICA)

Mental Welfare Commission for Scotland

Merseyside Partnership – Approved Social Workers

Lindsay Messenger – Solicitor – Mental Health Review Tribunal Panel Member

Paula Micallef – The UK Federation of Smaller M.H. Agencies

Middlesborough Council Social Services Department

Richard Mills – The National Autistic Society

MIND

Ministry of Health – Italy

Jane Mishcon – Barrister

Amanda Mortimer ASW – West Yorks Area

Peter Munn

Kevin Murray – Ealing, Hammersmith & Fulham NHS Trust

National Alliance of the Relatives of the Mentally Ill

National Institute for Social Work

National Schizophrenia Fellowship

National Self-Harm Network

Anna Navarro

R C Nessling – Bedfordshire Health Authority

Newcastle City Health Trust

The NHS Confederation

Norfolk County Council Social Services Department

Norfolk Women's Approved Social Workers Group

Northern Ireland Office

North Gwent Community Health Council

North Hampshire County Council – Social Services Department

Northamptonshire Approved Social Workers

North Lakeland Healthcare NHS Trust

North Tees Health NHS Trust

Lynda Oakley

Office of the Health Service Ombudsman

Guy Otten – Regional Chairman, Mental Health Review Tribunal
(Trent and Northern and Yorkshire Region)

Oxfordshire County Council – Social Services Department

Oxfordshire Learning Disability NHS Trust

Femi Oyebode – South Birmingham Mental Health NHS Trust

David Palmer

His Honour Henry Palmer

PAPYRUS

Mike Parker – Secretary – Rymni Valley MIND

Una Parker

Alan Parkin – Academic Director – University of Hull Law School

Elizabeth Parry – South Birmingham Mental Health NHS Trust

Susie Parsons – Chief Executive – Commission for Racial Equality

Partnerships in Care Limited

Jennifer Paul – Birmingham City Council – Social Services Department

Lisa Payne – National Children's Bureau

Louise Pembroke

Pembrokeshire and Derwen NHS Trust

Pembrokeshire Hearing Voices Group

Steve Picking

Elaine Powell – CARES

Roland Powell

Powys Health Care NHS Trust

Roger Pratt – Approved Social Worker

Roger Presswood

John Price – Patient Advocate – Nottingham Advocacy Group Ltd

Primary Care Development – Staffordshire University

PRiSM – Psychiatric Research in Service Management
Institute of Psychiatry

Prison Officers Association

Alison Prizeman

Radcliffes Solicitors

Mrs Vera Rago

Rampton Hospital Authority

Sir David Ramsbotham – HM Chief Inspector of Prisons

Joan Rapaport

Rev Nick Read – Rural Stress Information Network

Regional Chairmen – Mental Health Review Tribunal

Millie Reid – African Caribbean Mental Health Association

Peter Relton – Bradford Community Health

Revolving Doors Agency

Rhymni Valley MIND

Mag Richards – Powys Agency for Mental Health

Simon Richards – Assistant Director of Commissioning
Shropshire Health Authority

Sue Ricketts – Kaleidoscope

Jean Ritchie QC

Rochdale and District – Making Space

Brian Rogers – Community Psychiatric Nurses' Association

Dr Meera Roy – Consultant Psychiatrist – Black Country Mental Health NHS Trust

Royal College of Nursing – Nursing Forum for Learning Disability Nursing

Royal College of Psychiatrists

The Sainsbury Centre for Mental Health

Graeme Sandell – Head of Mental Health NACRO

SANE

John Sankey

The Schizophrenic Association of Great Britain

School of Community Health and Social Studies – Anglia Polytechnic & University

Baroness Scotland of Asthal QC

Peter Scott Blackman – AFIYA Trust

Scott Moncrieff, Harbour and Sinclair Solicitors

Section of Developmental Psychiatry – University of Cambridge

Rev Dr Peter Sedgwick – Board for Responsibility

Mr L C Sharpe – Care Programme Approach Association

Shropshire's Community & Mental Health Services NHS Trust

Jenny Shuttleworth – ASW West Yorks Area

Terry Simpson – United Kingdom Advocacy Network

Iain Sinclair – ASW West Yorks Area

Tim Skinner – Oxfordshire Social Services Department

Joan Sleight – ASW West Yorks Area

Andy Smith

Society for Individual Freedom

Society of Clinical Psychiatrists

Solihull Healthcare NHS Trust – Mental Health Services

Somerset County Council / Health Authority – Social Services Department

Somerset Joint Commissioning Team

Southampton Community Health Services NHS

South Birmingham Mental Health NHS Trust

South Downs Health NHS Trust

South Shropshire Community Mental Health Team

South Wales Mental Health Advocacy

South Warwickshire Branch of the Special Interest Group in Mental Health
British Association of Social Workers

South West London & St George's Mental Health Services NHS Trust

Penny Stafford

Staffordshire Social Services Department

Michael & Susan Standen

Benjamin M Stansfield – Kent Law Clinic

Dr Philip Sugarman – Trevor Gittens Unit – Kent Forensic Psychiatry Service

Surrey County Council Social Services

Surrey Oaklands NHS Trust

Survivors in Salford

Survivors of Mental Health Services in West Suffolk

Swansea MIND

Dr George Szmukler – Maudsley Hospital

Tameside Metropolitan Borough – Mental Health Team

Mary Taylor

Tees And East Yorkshire NHS Trust

Professor Edward E Tennant – The American University in London

Sean Llewellyn Terrell

Thames Valley Partnership

Ian Thomas – Monmouthshire Social Services Department

Liz Thorpe – TRIPOD

Dr David Tidmarsh

Dr David Torpy – Fromeside Clinic – Avon and West Wiltshire Trust

Neil Towe – Local Government Association

Trafford Social Services – Approved Social Worker

Adrian Treloar – Oxleas Trust

Heather Ann Trenchard – Mindlink
South and West National Advocacy Panel Member

Brian Tupman

David Turner & Co Solicitors

UK Acquired Brain Injury Forum (UKABIF)

UKAN

UKCC

UK Federation of Smaller Mental Health Agencies

UK Psychiatric Pharmacy Group

Ted Unsworth – Chief Executive – Turning Point

User Support Network

Values Into Action

Dr Eileen Vizard – Young Abusers Project
Camden & Islington Community Health Services NHS Trust

The Voices Forum – National Schizophrenia Fellowship

Dr Tony Wainwright – Cornwall Healthcare Trust

Gitta Wajntraub

Eryl Walters – Cheshire County Council Social Services Department

Ware & Peters Solicitors

J.A. Warren

Wells and District Group – National Schizophrenia Fellowship

Wessex Forensic Psychiatry Service

West Indian Standing Conference

Westminster Mental Health Advocacy Project

Wigan Metropolitan Borough Council – Social Services Department

Margaret Wilcox – Mental Health Manager – Shropshire Country Council

John Wilder – Psychiatric Rehabilitation Association

Alun Williams

Bryn Williams – Brecknock & Radnor – Community Health Council

Nikki Williams

Wiltshire Constabulary

Wiltshire and Swindon Users Network

Worcestershire Social Services Department – Working Party

Dr B Wright

R C Wrightmore

Dr A S Zigmond – Leeds Community & Mental Health Services
High Royds Hospital

Kilian Zumpe – City of Westminster Social Services Department